FLYING THE
RED DUSTER

FLYING THE RED DUSTER

A MERCHANT SEAMAN'S FIRST VOYAGE INTO THE BATTLE OF THE ATLANTIC 1940

Foreword by David Cesarani

MORRIS BECKMAN

SPELLMOUNT

First published 2011 by Spellmount, an imprint of
The History Press
The Mill, Brimscombe Port
Stroud, Gloucestershire, GL5 2QG
www.thehistorypress.co.uk

British Library Cataloguing in Publication Data.
A catalogue record for this book is available from the British Library.

ISBN 978 0 7524 5900 4

Typesetting and origination by The History Press
Manufacturing managed by Jellyfish Print Solutions Ltd.
Printed in India

CONTENTS

David Cesarani is an English historian specialising in Jewish history. His books include *Arthur Koestler: The Homeless Mind* (1998). In 2005 Professor Cesarani was awarded the OBE for 'services to Holocaust Education and advising the government with regard to the estabishment of Holocaust Memorial Day'.

FOREWORD BY DAVID CESARANI

When I was a boy growing up in a north London suburb I used to listen keenly to the stories told by a family friend, Eric, who used to visit our home every Monday night for a meal followed by *Panorama* on the television. He had been a merchant mariner and served on the Arctic convoys during the war. He didn't talk a lot about his experiences but something he said stuck in my mind. He recalled that if a ship was carrying timber the crew tended to sleep without wearing life jackets because, if hit by a torpedo, the vessel would stay buoyant long enough for them to get to the boat stations in good time. But if it was carrying iron ore they went to sleep ready to race for the lifeboats in seconds, which was all they would have if it was caught by a U-boat or bombed. As I lay in bed at night I tried to imagine what it was like to try to get to sleep on a freighter carrying explosives, inflammable petroleum products or bulk cargo. I shuddered at the thought.

In this gripping memoir of life as a merchant seaman, Morris Beckman repeats what I heard all those years ago – almost word for word. It was the lore of the Merchant Navy. But he has also filled in the silences and the gaps and with extraordinary skill he evokes what it was like to cross the Atlantic at the height of the battle for the sea lanes. This is the story of his first convoy, beginning with his training as a radio operator and his induction into the squalid conditions on a rusty old tanker, the SS *Venetia*. The crew was full of characters, each of whom is drawn with insight, compassion and humour. Morris writes unsparingly about the unsavoury personalities, poor pay and abysmal conditions. For much of the voyage, the crew's greatest enemy after the Germans was the crooked steward and the talentless cook.

On the journey to the Americas the convoy lost six ships. Morris, in the claustrophobic confines of the radio room, logged one distress signal after another from torpedoed merchantmen. He realised that to make the Atlantic run was to face 'sudden death without warning'. On the return leg the *Venetia* was loaded to the gunnels with high octane fuel; in effect they were sailing on a huge petrol bomb. One ship after another was hit and eleven were sunk before the convoy reached port. Even in British home waters there was a constant danger from mines, the Luftwaffe and E-boats – fast German Navy torpedo boats. No one reading this account will be able to avoid a quickening pulse as Morris brings the narrative to its climax.

Americans have long celebrated the veterans of the Second World War as 'the greatest generation'. In Britain, perhaps due to a tradition of modesty, for many decades we tended to play down the sacrifice and the achievements of the men and women who kept Britain free, liberated Europe and defeated fascism between 1939 and 1945. The Merchant Navy, which lost more than 34,000 officers and men, is amongst the least recognised of the services that took part in that struggle. Anyone seeking evidence of the horrors those men faced and the courage they displayed, need go no further than this frank and terrifying account.

Morris Beckman was just one member of a crew, on one ship in a succession of convoys, in a battle that lasted the entire war. But his story may stand for the stories of thousands. It is a fitting tribute to the greatest generation that ever sailed under the Red Duster.

Professor David Cesarani OBE
Royal Holloway, University of London

1

THE BATTLE OF THE ATLANTIC

The broad canvas.

The French capitulation in May 1940 enabled the Nazi *Kriegsmarine* to operate from ports stretching from the Arctic to the Mediterranean. From the newly acquired bases it had access to Britain's busiest sea routes, and the U-boats could make more sorties as they enjoyed shorter runs home for re-arming, re-servicing and provisioning. Their crews could recuperate for longer periods between forays into the Atlantic and the northern seas. The improvement in the performance of Admiral Dönitz's 'grey wolves' was immediate. In the first five months of 1940 the British lost 108 merchant ships with a gross tonnage of 408,810. In the last seven months of the year, after the Fall of France, they lost 440 with a gross tonnage of 2,026,857.

The British Merchant Navy operated in every theatre of the conflict. It ferried troops and supplies all over the world, took part in every sea-borne evacuation and invasion and suffered appalling losses on the Malta and Russian convoys. Yet all these peripheral activities took second place to the longest sea battle of the war, which covered an area larger than any other battle fought in Europe during the Second World War. It became known as the Battle of the Atlantic, and lasted from 3 September 1939 – when U-30 torpedoed SS *Athenia* en route from Liverpool to Montreal, with the loss of 117 lives – until 7 May 1945, when SS *Avondale Park* was sunk by U-*2336* an hour before the official German surrender. Often unprotected, a seaman of the merchant vessel convoys could do little as relentless fighting raged about him but do his job, pray, live with his lifejacket, and in the early days keep a condom waterproofing over his torch in case he found himself swimming after dark.

In 1941, with the tide of success running their way, Admirals Raeder and Dönitz pressed Hitler to build another 50 U-boats, but the request was denied. The Führer's obsession was with war on land, and after Dunkirk he had hopes that Britain would make peace with Germany. Had those 50 been built, Germany could well have won the war. As it was, in 1944 Hitler ordered the Kriegsmarine to commission 120 of the new, faster, long-range electric submarines. It was too late. By February 1945 only two had been built and the war was already lost.

Buoyed by success, the U-boat crews called the period between June 1940 and early 1943 their 'happy time'. It included that long year when Britain fought alone against the Axis powers and the Royal Navy was too thinly stretched to provide adequate escorts for convoys. Escorts lacked ship-borne radar and the enemy could only be spotted by the naked eye, often by the heart-stopping sight of a torpedo's wake as it headed for a ship. U-boats had learned to surface at night, rendering the escorts' underwater asdic detection system ineffective, and they were hard to spot when they sat low in the water under the cover of darkness. Fewer U-boats were being sunk than built; the Germans were ahead on tactics. And they had Admiral Dönitz.

Dönitz had been a successful U-boat commander during the First World War. He went on to make a study of underwater warfare, having never forgotten how the convoy system had frustrated and defeated the U-boats. He knew that if war came then the convoy system would again be employed, and he worked on how to counter it.

He instituted the *rudeltaktik* whereby his U-boats assembled and attacked convoys in groups of up to a dozen. To facilitate this he organised a communication system using shortwave radio which allowed U-boats at sea to communicate both with his headquarters at St Lorient and with each other. The submarines would operate in groups, each boat having its patrol line, and when one spotted a convoy it would stalk it for many days, giving the rest of the group time to converge and launch a pack attack. Thus, instead of losing the occasional ship to individual U-boat attacks, convoys could be practically wiped out. In October 1940, Convoy SC7 set out from Halifax, Nova-Scotia, heading for home. A 30-ship convoy, it was savaged on the nights of 16, 17 and 18 October. 19 vessels were lost. The 'wolf packs' decimated many other convoys, and the frightening losses of merchantmen were causing flutters in Whitehall. Winston Churchill admitted much later that the only thing that really frightened him was the U-boat peril.

The U-boat model doing the damage was the Type VIIC, which had a displacement of 872 tons and a surface speed of 17 knots. It could cruise at 10 knots for 10,000 miles and out-speed any convoy and the majority of lumbering merchant vessels. It carried 14 torpedoes, which could be fired from four tubes in the bows and from one tube aft. In addition it had two 2.20mm guns, one of which could be used as an anti-aircraft weapon. It was arguably the most efficient killing machine of the war.

German engineers and scientists ceaselessly devised new ways of sinking merchant vessels. In 1940 the Luftwaffe seeded the east coast of Britain with mines, from the Thames up to Tyneside. They alone destroyed 70 vessels. Then the Germans produced the magnetic mine which was attracted to ships passing overhead. The British countered this with an effective de-gaussing system which neutralised a ship's magnetic field. The Germans developed the acoustic mine, nicknamed the 'gnat', which was detonated by the vibrations from propellers.

Royal Navy minesweepers countered by trailing vibrators across the seas. Then the Kriegsmarine introduced the schnorkel which enabled U-boats to 'breathe' underwater, and the huge Type XIVs or *Milchkühe* (milk cows). These took up station in set positions in the mid-Atlantic, allowing operation U-boats to re-arm and take on provisions without returning to a land base.

Another effective German weapon was the Focke-Wulf Condor, a large plane with a range of nearly 2,500 miles and a bomb load of 4,620lbs. While they did attack Allied merchant vessels, their primary function was reconnaissance, spotting targets for their comrades underwater. They became a familiar sight to merchant seamen, and when the hated 'Angels of Death' appeared and circled round a convoy out of range of the ships' anti-aircraft guns, the seamen knew that their position, course, speed and numbers were being transmitted to the St Lorient headquarters, and that an attack was inevitable.

The British were not idle, and as well as the aforementioned anti-mine devices, they perfected a direction-finding receiver which could pinpoint the underwater position of a U-boat as it transmitted radio messages. The hunter-killer groups of Royal Navy corvettes and destroyers could home onto the submarine, and as a result U-boat losses climbed sharply. In response the Kriegsmarine forbade crews to chatter to each other at sea, but the hunter-killer groups continually devised new tactics to find their prey. The most successful group sank 25 U-boats and was led by Captain Frederick Walker, who won the DSO four times. Support also came from the air. By late 1943 Britain's coastal command had organised Sunderland and Catalina long-range aircraft into round-the-clock air cover. They were armed with radar and bombs, and patrolled areas round the convoys, forcing the U-boats to keep their heads down.

The most important British breakthrough was the deciphering of the German coding machine, Enigma. U-boat command used it to pass messages to the submarines, never imagining that it could be cracked. But it was, and it enabled the Royal Navy to divert convoys round the U-boat patrol lines and direct hunter-killer groups straight to their prey. This source of information, codenamed 'Ultra', was one of the war's greatest secrets.

The American entry into the war sealed the fate of the U-boat offensive. The US Navy took over the protection of ships along their eastern seaboard and their destroyers began to assist in the protection of Atlantic and Russian convoys. But the greatest American contribution to winning the Battle of the Atlantic was their incredible production of pre-fabricated deep sea cargo carriers. They were turned out by the hundreds and were called Liberty Ships.

It is estimated that the Atlantic and North Sea slogging match alone resulted in the loss of some 2,000 British merchant vessels and 27,000 officers and men. These figures do not include the Allied merchantmen lost, of which there were many thousands. They came from every Nazi-occupied country and were always in our convoys. Over the two-and-a-half years I spent on ship, I saw French, Polish, Greek, Dutch and Norwegian vessels attacked and their surviving crewmen lowering boats, throwing rafts overboard, and on what we called the 'flamers', frantically jumping into the freezing seas. The contribution of the merchantmen, both home-grown and foreign, was invaluable, especially at a time when Britain stood alone in Europe against a superior foe.

Before I joined the *Venetia*, I knew as much about the Merchant Navy as the average Briton – nothing. To me the merchant seaman was just a civilian plying his trade, albeit at sea rather than in a shop or office, but there was a difference between him and other men.

From the moment he boarded his ship until the day he walked ashore if and when his vessel returned home, he was under enemy attack. He was a sitting duck for all that the Luftwaffe and the Kriegsmarine could throw at him. His main pre-occupations were his grievances, low pay, poor food, the long weeks at sea and the very short breaks ashore. It was wartime and he knew that they had to be borne, but some were beyond the pale, such as the fact that if a ship was sunk, then the very same day the pay of the survivors was stopped by the shipping companies. It was a case of no ship, no work to be done, no wages. Protests by the National Union of Seamen and the Merchant Navy Officers Union were in vain. Patriotism was appealed to. It worked.

It was not uncommon for merchant seamen to encounter a particularly discomforting hazard. In seaport pubs seemingly healthy young men in civilian clothes would be taunted by others in uniform. The less they reacted to the taunts, the more outrageous they would become, especially if there were women present. The men subjected to the ridicule and accusations of cowardice – merchant seamen who had been torpedoed, mined, bombed and machine-gunned, suffered the heart-stopping antics of overloaded vessels in fierce gales and lived with the ever-present fear of seeing one of the Nazis' devastating battleships appear over the horizon – would be goaded into giving the uniformed 'heroes' their first battle wounds. I witnessed two such occasions, one in Avonmouth and one in Middlesbrough. Both times Royal Navy ratings joined in the fights alongside the merchant seaman.

To reduce these confrontations the Merchant Navy officers were issued with a lapel badge made from aluminium. It was roughly three-quarters of an inch long and half an inch deep. Inside the frame and stamped out in relief on the plate were the letters 'MN'. All this was surmounted by a clean anchor crown. By and large it was regarded by its recipients as an affront, a bad joke. Few wore it. It became known as the monkey-nut badge.

During my research I found tucked away inside the SS *Venetia*'s 'Agreement and List of the Crew' a booklet titled *Regulations for Maintaining Discipline*. After so many years its contents threw new light on the dissatisfactions and grumblings of a crew, who, all in all, did all that was asked of them, and more. At the time it was the practice that the master had it in his power to 'log' or fine men. These fines would be deducted from wages, which naturally was to the shipping company's advantage. Take into account the low wages, and a 'troublemaker' who was frequently logged could take home very little money at the end of a voyage. In the booklet the punishments were set out as follows:

1.	Striking or assaulting any other crew member	5 shillings
2.	Bringing on board intoxicating liquors	5 shillings
3.	Drunkenness 1st offence	5 shillings
	Drunkenness 2nd offence	10 shillings
4.	Taking on board any offensive weapon without concurrence of the Master	5 shillings for every day
5.	Insolent language or behaviour to Master or Officers or disobedience to lawful commands	5 shillings
6.	Absence without leave	5 shillings for every day.

Generally masters of vessels were reluctant to impose fines unless forced to do so by complete recalcitrants, who were usually drunk out of their minds.

Pay varied, but it was always low. The booklet laid down hard and fast overtime rates; men working in shifts were paid overtime for work done in excess of eight hours Monday to Friday, five hours on Saturday and all work done on Sunday.

Rates for overtime for boys	6 pennies per hour
Rates for overtime for ordinary seamen	6 pennies per hour
Rates for overtime for carpenters	1 shilling/ninepence per hour
Rates for overtime for other ratings	1 shilling/ninepence per hour

It was not much. But then, the men who manned Britain's forgotten wartime navy never wanted a lot, not even recognition.

2

TRAINING AND JOINING THE VENETIA

Max telephoned me the day after war broke out. We were close friends in and out of school. At Hackney Downs School he had been one of those enviable pupils to whom mathematics was a doddle. He was stubborn, dour and cynical. With two other friends we enjoyed cycling trips, rowed in a gig four on the river on Sundays and enjoyed the long Habonim summer camps. Now, out of character, he sounded ebullient.

'I'm coming round,' he said. 'I can't study anymore.'

From my home in Amhurst Road, Hackney, we walked to the RAF recruiting office in Kingsway, Holborn, and joined the short queue. The moment we reached the desk the heavily moustached corporal behind it growled lugubriously.

'Go back to bloody school and don't waste my time.'

Max bristled. He had a bristle that could change the atmosphere.

'Maybe you don't listen to the wireless or read the papers,' he retorted sarcastically. 'There's a war on and we want to fly.' The corporal waved a dismissive hand and snorted.

'It takes brains to fly an aeroplane. Just bugger off out of here. Go on! Hop it!' Studying the corporal as if he were something under a microscope, Max replied with great deliberation,

'So, it takes brains to fly an aeroplane does it? That must explain why you're sitting behind that desk!'

We shot out into the street. Max was now obsessed with flying. He dragged me round to other recruiting centres, but in vain. We were too young. It was too early. Things had to be organised. For three months we were lost souls and our studying for university suffered grievously. Then, while reading the *Daily Telegraph* one day, my eye caught one of the plethora of government notices that filled the newspapers in those days.

Admiralty notice. Radio officers urgently required for the Merchant Navy to maintain a continuous radio watch on all British ships at sea. Good pay. Good prospects. See the world.

I came to a snap decision. It was the invitation to see the world that did it.

Two days later I enrolled at a maritime college in an enormous converted Victorian house off Clapham Common. There I learned to transmit and receive Morse code at speed and across artificial interference, and how to service the heavy-duty marine transmitters and receivers. The very day the Phoney War ended and the Germans attacked France and the Low Countries, I was one of 52 students who took the examination and tests for our special certificates. Forty of us passed, and the next day we went to a famed eatery run by a dear old soul with hennaed hair and rouged cheeks who we called Fanny Bagwash. We celebrated with a slap-up lunch of steak and onion pie, two vegetables and Fanny's famed apple pie and custard.

The walls of Fanny's place were covered with hundreds of postcards from ports worldwide, sent by 'her boys' who had passed the course before us. The boisterous celebration came to a halt when Fanny burst into tears. The quick thinkers amongst us rushed to comfort her, and gave her the presents we had bought her – a box of Cadbury's

Milk Tray chocolates and 200 John Player cigarettes, for she enjoyed 'her pulls', as she called smoking. We then chaired her out into the street, down to nearby traffic lights and back into the café. To puzzled bystanders we announced it was her hundredth birthday. Once back inside she lined us up and kissed each of her boys on the cheeks, a mother bidding us farewell, and then we dispersed to every part of Britain. Over the next few years a name from that group of 40 would appear in the casualty section of the radio officer's monthly, *The Signal* as 'killed or missing'. Missing at sea meant dead.

The next day I took the bus to the Marconi office in East Ham High Street and signed onto their sea-going staff. I signed various forms, giving my next of kin as my father, Joseph Harris Beckman. He was a textile merchant and an immigrant from Poland, a devout Jew who could not come to terms with the youngest of his four sons being the first to leave. Max gave me hell for not having waited, like he did. He had joined the RAF and sported the white flash in his forage cap, denoting pilot training. He brimmed with enthusiasm about flying. Barely a year later Sergeant-pilot Maxwell Addess took off in his Hurricane from an East Anglian airfield. His squadron attacked a swarm of incoming German bombers and fighters. In the ensuing dogfight Max and his plane crashed into the sea. His body was never found.

I reported to the Marconi office day after day at 10am and went home at 5pm. I began to feel like a fraud as the sailor who had never been to sea. Those of us waiting for orders played cards and dominoes, read magazines and chatted about god-knows-what. Now and again a name would be called and the lucky man would cry out exultantly 'that's me!' He had his ship. Others who had completed voyages came into the office to collect pay and further instructions, or the statutory month survivor's leave. Our questions to them about what it was at sea like evoked dampening replies such as 'bloody awful', or a meaningful 'you'll soon find out'.

Came the morning my name was called. I was at the counter in a flash. The elderly clerk examined me over his pince-nez and smiled at my eagerness. It was my first ship, but he had sent hundreds of young men to sea. He gave me an advance of £25, which would be deducted from my pay, and then gave me a typed list of the sea-going gear I would need. He advised me to get it all from Gardiners, the famous old store which occupied an entire triangular site where Aldgate meets the East End. It was the specialist shop for all seafarers, British and foreign, and had a worldwide reputation. I went straight there and found it bustling with officers and seaman from several different military and merchant navies. It was all wood, the walls, floors, fitments, counters and shelving, which may have played a part in its eventual demise in the 1970s, when it was gutted by fire.

A telegram arrived the next morning, informing me that I had been appointed the second radio officer on the SS *Venetia*, anchored in the Thames. I was instructed to report to a Tilbury shipping office on the following day at 11am. Unable to sleep, I rose early, and caught a train from Liverpool Street station, finding myself in the designated office with time to spare. It was a dreary place in a desolate spot. The furniture was cheap, the grey walls dirty, and the notices pinned up were yellowed and curling at the edges. A forlorn-looking woman sat at a cluttered desk sorting through box files.

On the dot of 11am three men appeared. They were middle-aged and tweedy, ruddy and inclined to corpulence. They were the immigration officer, a Board of Trade official and the agent representing the shipping company. The latter smiled at me and said pleasantly:

'You're for the *Venetia*?'

'Yessir.'

'Good. We'll take you to it. We're doing the rounds.'

We all went out to a wide Daimler. It was roomy and had veneered wood panelling and leather seats. I sat in the back with my two suitcases. The three men sat up front, the agent driving us at a leisurely pace through the flat Thames Valley landscape. The officials stopped twice to refresh themselves, and judging by their conversation the barmaid in the second pub was far from unfriendly. We drove past a new estate of purple-bricked houses, past clusters of workmen preparing anti-invasion strong points and anti-aircraft gun positions. Once we were held up by a long column of marching infantrymen heading to the coast. I glimpsed the Thames between two stretches of high walls and then saw rows and rows of round metal containers the size of bungalows. The immigration official turned to me.

'That's your job sonny. To help keep those storage tanks topped up.'

The Daimler nosed through an entrance guarded by two soldiers in tin hats and carrying slung rifles, then we bumped across two railway lines. We passed through a no man's land of storage tanks and lean-tos, juddered across tangled rubber hoses and across another rail track. We swung round a long white-washed shack and there before us lay the Thames.

We all clambered out of the car. I walked to the edge of the quayside, my shoes splashing in patches of oil. Water slapped against the stone blocks of the wall. I heard the creaking of ropes strained between bollards on the quayside and the boats below, the distant clanking of metal hitting metal and the incessant shrieking of the swooping seagulls. There was that indefinable tang where salt water meets land, of canvas and tar, seaweed and refuse.

Anchored in mid-stream lay the SS *Venetia*. I drank in the sight of her. She was rust-streaked and dowdy, low slung with one grimy squat runnel aft. Patches of red lead chequered her grey plates. She pulled gently at the anchor chain that dropped taut from her bows. She resembled a dilapidated toy in a junk shop window, but she was a tanker with half a million miles under her hull. Only the advent of war had saved her from the scrap yard. I wondered how a ship which looked so small and frail could cross oceans. The agent put his hand on my shoulder.

'Joining your first ship can be a depressing business. I went through it myself some years ago. You'll perk up once you get on board. You'll have to because the merchant service is now a top priority, essential service, and you'll be in it for the duration.' He shook my hand. 'Bear in mind, laddie, that every ship which brings home a cargo wins a victory, a small one perhaps but as important as any won by the armed forces. Good luck.'

Twenty feet separated the top of the quay from the boats below. A vertical steel ladder, its rungs cemented into the stonework, was the only means of descent. An open boat with a small engine aft bobbed up and down at its foot. A blue-jerseyed boatman was holding it close to the ladder with a boathook. I gripped one of my cases in my left hand and gingerly lowered myself over the edge. I descended fearfully, the tide lines in the stonework darkening as I climbed down. The high rungs were burnished and smooth, then they roughened, and as I came closer to the waterline they became slippery underfoot. I heard the profound truism that some mothers do have 'em. I looked down at the greenish scum in the margin where the river met the wall, saw the boat and jumped, landing in it with my case on top of me. The boatman shook his head;

'What a performance. Lucky there's no rigging nowadays for you to climb. Now, hurry up and get the other case. I've got more jobs to do.'

I managed my second journey a trifle more quickly. We pushed off and the feeling of the breeze and spray on my face was invigorating. I saw another launch deposit my three companions at the *Venetia*'s gangway, which they ran up with their briefcases like athletes. My boat approached and just when I thought we were going to ram her, the boatman swung the wheel and we bumped alongside the platform at the gangway's foot. I turned to him.

'How much do I owe you?' He shook his head.

'The company pays for this one, but if you want to come ashore again it will cost half a crown.'

22

I managed to land myself and my cases onto the gangway platform. I was wearing my brand new uniform and cap and had felt as mint as an unopened packet of cigarettes, but under the hot sun I was afloat in perspiration. I looked up and saw four amused weather-beaten faces peering down at me. I cringed with self-consciousness. A fifth face, gaunt and priestly, joined them, followed by a sixth which looked simian yet dependable, a seventh with the straight black hair and roundness of a Celt, a fair-haired young eighth and a ninth, as ruddy as a tomato and Saxon-thatched. I struggled up the gangway with my two cases, steadfastly not looking up, because I knew that they knew I was joining my first ship. A seaman came down with maddening ease and agility, and whisked my two cases onto the well-deck. I followed as my helper, a stock blonde ape of a man with long arms, quipped,

'Blimey they're heavy. What's in them? Your winter woollies?' The welcoming heads, now attached to bodies stripped to the waist or in working dungarees, crowded round, bantering and teasing.

'Can I polish your nice shiny buttons, sir?'

'What a smart uniform!'

'I hope you've made your will, matey...'

I had never been so nonplussed. What to do? Answer back? Keep quiet? Walk away? But where to? Then I was rescued. A fair and wiry youth of my own age, wearing blue overalls and a peaked black cap set at a jaunty angle, scattered the welcoming party by waving a marlin spike at them with mock lethal intent. He did so with good humour, to which they responded, and then returned to their duties. He held out his hand to me and we had a long firm handshake.

'You're the new Sparky?' I nodded. 'I'm the apprentice, the ship's dogsboy. I'm Johnny Walters. Call me Johnny.'

'I'm Morris Beckman. Call me Morris...'

'No.' Johnny smiled and shook his head. 'You are Sparky.' And that was my name ever afterwards. I expressed thanks at his having turned up when he did. 'They're a good bunch. You just happened to be a heaven-sent diversion. Being stuck on this rust bucket for weeks on end with very little shoreside is bloody monotonous.'

He picked up my larger case and told me to follow him. He wondered out loud why I hadn't tried for a better ship.

'Is she as bad as all that?'

'Bad? The British Merchant Navy has the bummest tramps afloat. The company has the bummest ships in it, and we're the worst ship in the company.'

'Can't *you* apply for another ship?' Johnny shook his head dolefully.

'No. I'm apprenticed until my articles expire. When I pass my second mate exam and become a certified deck officer then I can try for other ships in other companies.'

The exciting smell of canvas and paint, tar and hot metal, permeated everywhere. Tanned and stripped to the waist, ordinary and able seamen were chipping, red-leading, painting and doing mysterious things with thick coils of rope. A group were heating tar in a small cauldron and re-caulking worn down joins between the areas of deck planking. Johnny led me up a short companionway into the lower amidships accommodation. Six cabins, three to each side, opened onto the narrow central alleyway. Johnny opened the door to one of the two nearest the entrance. It was about half the size of a box room in an average suburban house. He executed a Gallic bow and flourish.

'Voila M'sieur Sparky. It is all yours. Could be smaller, but not much.'

The bulkheads and deckhead had once been cream, but they badly needed re-painting and were patterned with the dried-out remains of hundreds of cockroaches and other seafaring insects. A limp cobweb dangled in a corner, the brass fittings were pitted with rust, and the small sink was a network of grease-filled cracks held together by veined porcelain. Over everything hung the odour of filth. I forced open the three narrow drawers of the dressing table. They gave up rusty nails, torn girly magazines, a broken knife, part of an epaulette and a photo of a naked senorita on her back waving her legs in the air. I ran my fingers along the edge of the bunkboard; they came away black. I opened the small door covering the pipes under the washbasin, and found the place swarming with cockroaches.

'God. Who was the last occupant? A pig?'

'Not quite what you're used to?' grinned Johnny. 'With a good clean out she'll be a palace. Later this afternoon I'll help you to soogie it out.'

'Soogie?'

'We pour loads of crystal soda into boiling water and then scrub like mad.' He glanced at his watch. 'The mate will want me, I must go. Don't lift up your mattress. You'll find the bunkboard underneath full of creepy crawlies. Better go and introduce yourself to Smith, he's your chief. He's been on the *Venetia* longer than I have, always on his own.'

Out on deck the brass and steel reflected the sun's heat even more intensely, and my shirt and underwear were wringing sweat. There was the odour of the sort of cooking which wafts through pavement grills outside bad restaurants. Hands were working inside the two lifeboats, one to port and the other to starboard of amidships. Hands were busy everywhere. The older a ship becomes the more attention she needs, and the *Venetia* was a lady nearing her grave.

I saw the aerial stretched between the mast tops and looked down its lead-in to the radio cabin. It was protected by four thicknesses of sandbags, leaving only the door free. Inside, bent over a conglomeration of radio components was a trim figure in spotless white dungarees. I coughed. No answer. I coughed again. The man I took to be Smith continued to probe the leaves of a condenser with a screwdriver. I said in a low voice that I was the new man reporting for duty.

'Really!' Smith straightened up and turned. He was tall, fair-haired and quizzical. He stared at me. Discomfited I ventured;

'This is my first ship. Not bad is she?'

'If it's your first, how do you know?'

'Er… I supposed so.'

'Supposed?' He frowned. 'You either know or you don't know. You never suppose. Understand?'

I nodded. His thin ascetic face with hair brushed straight back along a narrow skull broke into a faint smile. He extended a hand, small with tapering fingers, but with a strong, dry grip. 'I've been on my own for so long I've grown to like it. I hope we get on well together. Now take off that heavy jacket and we'll go over the equipment.'

This we did. Then he made me tap out a long message on the dead Morse key; its transmitter was not on. He listened intently, deciphering the words from the clicks. He then switched on the receiver and tuned it to 600 metres and watched me write down what I heard. Local interference and nervousness meant I made a few mistakes. He said I would have to practise until I made none.

'We're making ready for sea. The captain is ashore with the company's agent. Lunch will be late. You'd better see about it for yourself.'

I was glad to escape the gloom and humidity of the radio cabin. As I leaned on the rail enjoying the sunshine, Johnny came and leant next to me.

'Grub's up Sparky.'

'Funny. I don't feel all that hungry.'

'No problem. You won't eat it when you see it. I eat purely to annoy the chief steward. The more I eat the less money he makes for himself. It's a Merchant Navy tradition that pursers and chief stewards make more money than ships' captains. If they don't then they're no good at their jobs.'

The saloon was a square with a 30-foot side. Oak-panelled bulkheads gave it the cosiness of a country inn. There were three framed landscape prints, two portraits of Their Majesties, a chronometer and bookshelves containing a selection reminiscent of a boarding house. It was centred on a solid mahogany table, which had electric fans fixed to each corner and was flanked by chairs. Both table and chairs were bolted to the deck. The mate, second mate, Smith and Johnny were at the table when I entered, already eating. I waited to be allotted a chair, but as no one bothered I slid into the nearest empty one.

They all stopped eating. Expressions ranged from amusement to astonishment. Stevey, the assistant steward, a burly pugilist whose soup-spilling at anchor gave promise of exciting meals ahead, threw me a heavy wink over the chief officer's head. The latter, a portly Liverpudlian called Mr Parkinson, shook his head and said genially

You've done well, lad. Your first day at sea and you've made captain before me. That seat belongs to Mr Michaels and no one else.'

I learned later that Mr Parkinson did in fact have his master mariner's certificate, and had captained cargo-passenger ships for many years before retiring to cultivate a lucrative nursery garden. The war had brought him back to sea; he wanted to do his bit.

Roy Garrett, the second mate, an Australian from Melbourne, piped up.

'Tradition has it, Sparky, that if mates can't have their skipper's seats then they make darned sure no one else gets them.' There was laughter. I hastily took the empty chair between Johnny and Roy. The meal was terrible, consisting of carrot soup which was metallic to the taste, followed by what could have been grass cuttings and plasticine. This was eulogised as 'sea pie'. The dessert was a yellow mound of soggy dough covered with custard, which the cook said was Thames Duff. The same dessert was to become Texan Delight in Galveston, Abadan Flan in the Persian Gulf, and ammunition to be aimed at bum boats in the Suez Canal. I had a few sips of the soup, left the main course and finished off the duff. My companions cleaned their plates. Roy nudged me and warned 'the food is really good now. It deteriorates when we get to sea.'

Back in my cabin, I sat down on the narrow settee, which was lumpy and smelled distinctly unpleasant. Having dined unsatisfactorily I was hungry, and decided to fill up on water. The tumbler provided was too dirty to use, its bottom encrusted with brown sediment. I turned on the tap and caught water in my cupped hands. It came out brownish and speckled with bits. Closer inspection revealed them to be fragments of insects. Utterly dejected, I sank back on the settee and wondered what the hell I was doing there.

There was a knock at the door; it was Johnny and Stevey with three buckets of hot water, two large packets of soda, three scrubbing brushes and several cloths.

'Take off your jacket and shirt, Sparky,' said Stevey. 'If we get stuck in you'll be sleeping in a clean cabin tonight.' We went at it with such a will that we all got soaked with the soda water. We did not leave a nook or cranny untouched. When Stevey lifted the mattress he revealed a carpet of animated cockroaches, and found insects and slugs in the mattress itself. He said he would get rid of it and get me a new one. He was as good as his word, returning later with a new mattress, two sheets, two flattish pillows, two blankets, a large and a small towel, soap, a bottle of Dettol disinfectant and a clean glass tumbler. That night, exhausted, starving and still disorientated, I fell into a deep sleep.

Johnny, on the other hand, did not. All the time he was helping me he was distracted by thoughts of a girl called Rita, who he had wanted to be ashore with that night. Later, when we had become close friends, he told me all about it. Johnny's home was in Portobello, near Edinburgh. He was the only child of comfortably off parents; his mother was a solicitor and his father was a master mariner, and they were both against him going to sea. They had wanted him to become articled to a substantial law firm, the chairman of which was a family friend. But Johnny was stubbornly set on a maritime career, and after a series of searing rows with his son, Johnny's father had given in and arranged for his indenture as an apprentice to Gow, Harrison and Company. Since then my friend had only had a few days leave after his first trip and a week off in February 1940. He had been told that after the *Venetia* returned on the voyage just ended he would be replaced and have ten days leave to see his mother, with whom he was very close, and he had been looking forward to those ten days the entire trip.

There was an even more pressing reason for Johnny to see his mother. Early in March she had been widowed. Her husband had been the captain of a San boat, a larger tanker than the *Venetia*. On the way home in a Bermuda convoy she took two torpedoes and in minutes was burning from stem to stern. Escaped oil set the sea alight, and only a handful of survivors were picked up by an escort ship, most of them badly burned.

One, the third mate, knew Johnny and his family. He told my friend that his father had been so intent in seeing if anyone aboard needed help that he delayed jumping over the side until it was too late. He jumped into a circle of water surrounded by flames. The third mate, clinging to a raft some twenty yards away, saw him trapped, then a gust of wind blew the fire over him and he was gone. Johnny had asked him if his father had shouted or called out. The third mate refused to reply at first, and then sighed, saying that he had screamed, just that. He added that he himself was screaming continually with the pain of the salt water in his burns, which meant he needed skin grafts on his body, arms and face. He doubted that he would ever go back to sea. Johnny never told his mother of the encounter.

When the *Venetia* had entered the Thames estuary a couple of days before I joined her, Mr Michaels called Johnny to his quarters.

'I knew your father well. He was a fine man and a great loss to all who knew him. When I was ashore in Bermuda for a convoy conference I sent a telegram to the office saying that I wanted a replacement for you, so that you could have two weeks leave with your mother. Don't bank on it, but maybe…'

Johnny banked on it. He had to hope. But when the ship's mail arrived Mr Michaels called Johnny to him with bad news. 'Sorry, laddie. Office can't replace you and in view of the fact that we're due for instant turn-around you can't make Edinburgh.' He told Johnny to go to London for two days to enjoy himself. Johnny went. His phone calls to his disappointed mother and the pain in her voice almost unhinged him.

He met a young girl called Rita. They spent the night together in a small hotel by Liverpool Street station, and in the morning she went off to work in a Stepney clothing factory, but not before they arranged to meet that evening. He rang his mother again and they talked about his father. She cried into the telephone, and he thought of his solid, phlegmatic father screaming in the sea. He'd had enough. He went back to the hotel, paid his bill, packed his bags and returned to the *Venetia*. That night, lying on his back staring at the steel deckhead, he thought of Rita and could have cried himself.

3

THE WAITING GAME

On Tuesday 23 July 1940 I was woken by Stevey at 7am. He did this by pulling the blanket and sheet off me.

'Wakey wakey,' he yelled joyously. 'Breakfast at 7.30 sharp. Put on your blues. The Old Man is aboard and if he comes down for breakfast and finds someone not properly dressed they are for it.'

Starving, I was in the saloon on the dot. The mate, Roy and Johnny were already there, and we were joined by Smith. He told us to our relief that the 'Old Man' was breakfasting in his quarters. There were two large filled teapots, milk and sugar on the table. Stevey brought in bowls of porridge, nourishing if not very tasty. Then came the eagerly awaited main course of one egg, one sausage, bacon and baked beans. I ate the egg and beans, but morosely forked the bacon and sausage around the plate. Oh God, the handicap of being born Jewish and having had a religious upbringing, albeit forced. Roy oozed crocodile sympathy as he nudged me;

'Problem, Sparky? I'll help you out.' He demolished my bacon and stared hungrily at the sausage. 'You can't eat that, it's pork.' I told him to take the bloody thing, which he did. 'The bread is great, fresh-baked and there's butter and blackcurrant jam – delicious sandwiches you can stuff yourself with,' he advised consolingly. I picked out two doorstop slices of bread, which was crusty and smelled quite

31

good. Then I noticed the black specks. I asked Roy what they were. He patted my shoulder and said, 'nothing to worry about, Sparky. They're just bits of careless cockroaches that got caught in the dough. They're full of protein. Very healthy.' I put them back.

I swiftly became less fussy. Two weeks later I was nibbling small pieces of bacon between slices of bread. This worried Roy. I offered to swap my bacon for his egg. No dice. He just had to have his egg. Four weeks later, after apologies to Jehovah and Dad, I was eating quite sizeable pieces and Roy sighed over my chances of reaching heaven.

At midday a new crew signed on the *Venetia* for the coming voyage. Forty-eight of us formed a loose queue stretching from the saloon back along the flybridge almost to the gun platform aft. There were the three deck officers and Johnny, four engineers and two radio officers. There was the carpenter, referred to as Chippy, the boatswain, abbreviated to 'bosun', the cook and his galley boy. There was the chief steward and his assistant, Stevey, and a young steward for the engineers' accommodation aft. He was an irrepressible Irish-Liverpudlian know as Billy Boy.

There was also the DEMS marine sergeant and one Royal Marine. DEMS stood for Defence Equipped Merchant Ships. Royal Navy personnel were seconded to merchant vessels to man the antique guns de-mothballed for the war, and to train merchant seamen in their handling, in case, as a Welsh seaman put it, we sighted the *Tirpitz* battleship and needed to sink her. The *Venetia*'s 4-inch gun was sited aft on a circular gun platform and could swivel around 180 degrees and be elevated and lowered.

These were the specialists and executives who directed the ordinary and able seamen and the donkeymen greasers manhandling the *Venetia* and her cargo across the oceans. We belonged to eight different nationalities and came from various walks of life. Yet, while we served aboard the *Venetia*, hardship and danger would compress us into shipmates, happy or at strife with one another as temperament and circumstances would dictate. Our separate tasks would dovetail into working the ship. Our comfort and lives would be interdependent. The careless flash of a torch after dark, the slow reaction of the helmsman or the slackness of a lookout could kill us all.

I was near the end of the queue and waited patiently. After signing on there was nothing to do, nowhere to go. I recollected Samuel Johnson paralleling the seaman's lot with that of a jailbird, with the latter having the advantage of not risking his life. The elderly white-haired man in front of me kept hawking into a large soiled handkerchief. It made me a little queasy. I asked the man behind me who he was.

'Maltese Johnny. Our cook.'

'Sorry I asked.'

'Adds flavour, man. So you're the new Sparky.' We shook hands. 'I'm Dai Beaser, pig iron polisher in gold braid. Fifth engineer.'

Dai was from Merthur Tydfil. He was short, stocky and loquacious. Talk bubbled from him uncontrollably. Poverty had driven him from school down the mines at an early age, and recession had cost him his job and put him on the dole. He had always been good at fixing cars and machinery, so when he failed to find work locally he went to see a boyhood friend who was an engineer on a grain carrier in Avonmouth. A vacancy for a greaser on his friend's ship arose and Dai grabbed at it. He did not lack ambition, and decided to study, pass exams and climb up the long ladder to becoming a chief engineer. I asked him if he liked the sea.

'Ashore I'd have been back on the dole. Now I've got a career. But, I don't like being on this bastard.' I wondered why. 'Why?' he exclaimed. 'Apart from her plates being worn so think you can poke a knitting needle through them and when she hits weather she rolls enough to make cheese, don't you know?' I shook my head. 'We're on a tanker, not a dirty tanker which carries safer heavy oils, lubricants and molasses, but on a clean tanker. Petrol, three thousand tons of it,

Sparky, that's what we're going for. Hope we carry 80 octane and not 100 octane...'

'What's the difference between the octanes?

'About 2,000 feet higher on the 100 octane if we get hammered.' I wished I'd not asked. Dai added consolingly, 'Don't worry about it though. If it happens we won't know much about it.'

The signings took place at the saloon table before the mate, the chief steward – known cruelly as 'Twitch' because his face had a convulsive tic which took some getting used to – the company's representative and his clerk. Maltese Johnny signed the enormous register after some enthusiastic nib-licking which put as much ink on his tongue as on the paper. Then it was my turn. I wrote down my personal data in places indicated by the mate's calloused thumb, then it was done. I was now legally committed to making the voyage. There could be no retraction except through illness. I felt content. The die was cast and all I had to do henceforth was my job. Out on deck I watched a tight formation of three Spitfires flash by overhead. I went into the radio cabin and practised on a dead key. I wanted to increase my speed and accuracy of transmission.

Lunch was a disaster. It comprised plates of sandwiches and two bowls of very limp salad. As I did not eat ham and was allergic to cheese, I made do with plum duff and lumpy custard. Later, I was in my cabin reading the diagrammatic manuals on our radio equipment given to me by Smith, when Stevey appeared with a large mug of tea and two chocolate wafers.

'I noticed you didn't eat much at lunch,' he said self-consciously. He was a square man in body, with a square head set into square shoulders. Even his stubby fingers were squared off at the tips. His ugly, city-sharp face exuded pleasure as I ate and drank. It was an act of kindness I never forgot. Later, a very disconsolate Johnny appeared and plumped down on my settee muttering 'bastard' over and over again.

'What's up?'

'We're not sailing for another five days. I could have gone home instead of wasting a day in London.' I had never seen him so bitter. It was then that he told me about his day in London and about his father and his mother's disappointment. We were the same age. It was comforting that we could bank on being able to confide in and support one another.

For five days the *Venetia* lay at anchor. The mate and Roy wisely found plenty of work for idle hands. They had them painting and scraping the accommodations and over the side in cradles. I wandered aft and the two marines were delighted to show me how to fuse shells and work the gun. Dai took me down into the engine room to see what he lovingly called his 'load of old iron'. Johnny kept slipping into my cabin when he wanted to keep out of the mate's line of sight.

I read copiously and became acquainted with several members of the crew. I struck up an especially close friendship with a Spanish able seaman called Pablo Valdez. He was sunbathing on the focsle head, playing with a miniature chess set as he followed a book filled with games by chess grandmasters. I had always played at home with my three brothers and Pablo was delighted to find an opponent. He told me that he had been a communist and a left wing journalist who had written articles denouncing Franco and fascism. He had fought against Franco, and when the Republican armies collapsed he had escaped through Perpignan to France. He dared not return to Spain, and after kicking his heels in southern France he signed on a British ship in Marseilles and had worked on British ships ever since.

Urged on by Smith I practised transmitting on a dead key and checked over the ten wooden boxes containing the many-celled wet batteries on 'monkey-island', the roof of the wheelhouse. I checked the specific gravity of each cell and topped up with distilled water as needed. Then I scraped all the terminals and connections linking the batteries in series, and checked that the insulators were well fastened and clean.

I also did a great deal of exploring of the *Venetia*. Her construction was as follows: her hull comprised the long cavity filled with storage tanks stretching from the forepeak right back to the engine room cavity aft, from which rose the stubby round funnel. Two longitudinal bulkheads ran the entire length of the storage capacity. Transversal bulkheads sectionalised the three rows of tanks. They also reduced the area for flooding in case the hull was holed. From stem to stern the storage and engine room were covered by the steel well-deck, which was broken up by the engine room skylights, tightly screwed down tank covers and ventilators, each the height of a man.

There were three main accommodations: the focsle or more correctly fo'c's'le (abbreviation for forecastle), the amidships, set well back to give a long stretch of well-deck forward and the accommodation aft. A wooden yard-wide flybridge, ten feet above the well-deck, ran the entire length of the ship. It had a rope lifeline from end to end. This was threaded through the eyes of iron stanchions situated two yards apart.

Thirty-three seamen, oilers and donkeymen-greasers lived in the focsle in the most arduous conditions with no privacy. Living quarters in focsles like that on the *Venetia* had been condemned by the seamen's union and others. As late as 8 July 1938 Lady Astor, speaking in the House of Commons, condemned the fact that British seamen were underpaid and lived in filth. A Conservative MP who visited London docks commented that he would not put a ferret where some seamen lived on some of the ships. The *Venetia* was such a ship.

Conforming to the lines of the bows, the focsle was spade-shaped. Its one entrance at the wide end gave out onto the well-deck. Its heavy wooden doors opened inwards and in bad weather were protected by a stormboard comprising inch-thick planks that slotted either side into two vertical iron grooves. The residents said the planks kept them imprisoned and made some claustrophobic. Inside the focsle the deck rose towards the stem so that in one third of the space the men had to crouch to move about. On both bulkheads were clamped two tiers of metal bunks. Barely an inch of metal separated sleepers from the sea without, and a torpedo strike would have resulted in horrific loss of life, such was the limited protection. In the tropics the whole area became an oven, plagued with flies and cockroaches; those off-watch preferred to sleep on deck. When gales raged outside and the portholes were closed and the ventilators canvassed off, it reeked of rubberised clothing, wet wool and body odour.

The residents of the focsle lived under a cloud of tobacco smoke; the old hands said it was antiseptic and anathema to the cockroaches. They had the use of two outside wooden huts with metal framework, which covered four toilets and four showers. When the sea was swamping the well-deck many thought it was better to be constipated rather than drowned.

The amidships accommodation comprised three square boxes, one atop the other, in a pyramid shape. At well-deck level was the saloon, its adjoining pantry and storeroom, two lavatories and a spacious washroom with a white enamelled bath and two showerheads. There were also cabins for the three deck officers, Johnny, myself and the chief steward. The latter had the largest cabin by far, as it also served as his office.

The next level up, the lower bridge, was made up of the captain's large quarters, Stevey's cabin adjoining it – a large part of his duties was to look after the captain's needs – the radio cabin and Smith's cabin next to that. A narrow promenade deck surrounded the whole level. The final level above comprised the wheelhouse, the chartroom and two glass enclosed windows. In the wheelhouse were binoculars, two voice tubes connected to the engine room and the radio cabin, a phone line linked to the DEMS gunners aft and a board showing engine revolutions. There was also an aldis lamp for the visual signalling of planes and other ships, a loud-hailer, barometer and chronometer. The roof of the wheelhouse was the deck of monkey-island, an open space enclosed by wooden walls four feet high. Apart from the batteries mentioned above, it also supported a binnacle with compass behind the emergency steering wheel, twin Lewis guns with their boxes of ammunition, and a direction-finding aerial. Two companionways, one to port and the other to starboard, lined the three levels.

The aft accommodation held the chief engineer's quarters, individual cabins for his four engineers and a cabin each for the bosun, cook and Chippy (the carpenter). The latter had his workshop adjoining his quarters. The steel galley by the foot of the funnel was an oasis of warmth in the icy northern seas and an unbearable Turkish bath in the tropics. Right aft, perched on the poop, was the steel gun platform and the gun. The two marines – a grizzled sergeant and a callow recruit – shared a sturdy metal-framed wooden cabin next to their charge. In heavy seas they did not walk out of it so much as swim. They never complained.

On the sixth day of lying at anchor I had an overwhelming urge to get ashore, if only to walk without being confined by ship's rails. Smith gave me permission and I asked Johnny to accompany me, but he declined. He had become very morose, which was completely out of character. He had been on a hard roll of work and studying and still felt bitter about his aborted long leave. He gave me a thick letter to post to his mother.

I caught a liberty boat ashore for half a crown and caught a taxi into Grays. My first stop was a cafe where I lunched on minestrone soup, eggs, tomatoes, baked beans and chips, followed by apple pie and custard. It was paradise. Afterwards I walked for miles, booked into a bed and breakfast for the price of two pounds, went to the cinema and saw a western, and had a dinner of steak and chips.

After the meal I was caught in the mariner's age-old dilemma – what to do on a solitary night in an out-of-the-way place, knowing nobody? Music and laughter coming from a corner pub drew me like a moth to a flame. It was packed with civilian air defence and service personnel. A group of soldiers sang with great gusto and minimum harmony round a woman pianist pounding a honky-tonk piano. Local girls and soldiers from nearby gun sites were heavy petting in corners. A young woman rested her hand on my shoulder.

'I haven't seen you before. Why aren't you in uniform?' she asked suspiciously.

'I'm in the Merchant Navy.'

'Oh.' She nudged her soldier companion and said 'get him a drink.' The man returned with a pint of bitter, which I had never drunk before. We clinked glasses. They swigged while I sipped; I disliked the taste but it made me sociable. I talked to strangers, joined in the singing and at closing time I left arm in arm with a buxom blonde matron called Winnie and a toothy air raid warden. The latter kept turning round and yelling

'Watch the blackout! Keep those curtains pulled tightly, don't shine torches and don't smoke! Jerry can spot a cigarette lighter from 5,000 feet up!' I wondered how he knew that. He shook my hand, she gave me a smacking kiss, and they departed. I was left wandering around the chill blacked-out streets wishing I was back on the *Venetia*. Miraculously I stumbled across a cafe where I found two of my shipmates, Harry Reed, the third engineer, and a young greaser. With the amiable improvidence of the seafarer they had missed the last transport back. I sneaked them into the room I had booked; Harry slept on the settee while the greaser sprawled by the door. Unfortunately the landlady's daughter tripped over him when she brought me my morning tea. Having run downstairs in a panic, she returned with her mother, who told us amiably that we could come down for three breakfasts, which we would have to pay for, but that she wouldn't charge my friends for their impromptu lodging.

Via bus and taxi we reached Heaven's End and climbed down into the launch to take us back home. Just as the boatman was about to pull away a voice hailed us from the quay above.

'Wait, boatman!'

It was an incisive voice, one used to be obeyed, and sure enough the boatman held the launch to the ladder. An elderly man in a dark navy raincoat and matching trilby, clutching a document case and a holdall, clambered nimbly down the ladder and joined us in the boat. Harry Reed whispered in my ear,

It's Mr Michaels, our skipper. He's an old shellback. He served his apprenticeship in the last of the sailing clippers and thinks engines are messy and that engineers are a pain in the arse.'

The new arrival greeted us in the thickest of Scottish accents and looked every inch a seadog. More than fifty years of exposure to sun and wind had wrinkled and crinkled his hairless pate into seamed leather. Two hard eyes peered from under snow-white bushy eyebrows. He stared at me.

'You are our new radio officer, I presume.'

'Yessir.' He nodded.

'Good, good.'

That evening a small convoy of coasters steamed past the *Venetia*, outward bound, some loaded down to their plimsoll lines and others, in ballast, riding high. The bosun watched the parade with me, a Bristolian whose real name I never learned, who had been at sea since his early teens, and now, in his mid-forties, was the lynchpin between the deck officers and the seamen. He ceaseless checked that all was shipshape, was unflappable and solid, and Roy described him as the most valuable man on board.

He nodded at the fourth ship of the convoy, which was savagely pock-marked about her superstructure.

'When France fell, Sparky, it put the Merchant Navy into no man's land. Now, nowhere at sea is safe at any time. Not even in port.'

A tangible restlessness pervaded the *Venetia*'s officers and men. We were all heartily sick of living at anchor. When four bells rang I put on my uniform for dinner, having been forewarned by Stevey that it would be expected given Mr Michaels' presence. The latter sat at the head of the table, his head hunched into his shoulders and his keen eyes darting everywhere. Johnny was not at table, being on watch, but the acting third mate was present. Ian Mcpherson was twenty and from Aberdeen, making his last trip, so he hoped, as an uncertificated officer. He would sit for his second mate exam on our return. He was tall and gangly, and had outgrown his uniform, his sleeves showing a few too many inches of wrist. In temperament he was quiet, humourless and very stubborn. His shyness contributed to his not being liked by the seamen.

Stevey served the meal with his usual perilous enthusiasm. He came from Portsmouth, a likeable rogue without peer as teller of tall tales. So far he had informed me of his exploits mining for gold in Rhodesia, driving a taxi in Vancouver, promoting boxing in Manchester, finding opals in Columbia and an escape from a New South Wales bush fire.

Mr Michaels' presence dampened down the usual dinner banter. As we sipped coffee he rapped the table and announced that we would sail on the morrow.

'Jesus,' exclaimed Roy, 'thank bloody Christ.' Ian glowered at him. He was a devout Presbyterian. Stevey, who liked to be first with news, even if he had to make it up, hurried out to tell the crew.

The next morning, as I leaned on the rail staring at the shore, an addictive pastime for men at sea, I mused that for the first time I would be doing a useful job. My reverie was broken by a stentorian shout from the upper bridge on the loud hailer.

'All set forward?'

'All set forward,' Johnny confirmed from the focsle head. He issued orders to Chippy and the two seamen by the windlass. Chippy hammered away a holding belt and pulled a lever and the windlass stuttered into life. The bridge telegraph tinkled, evoking acknowledgement from the engine room, and a rhythmic thrumming spread outwards through the *Venetia*. She came alive, no longer an inert mess of pig iron. The oil tanks of Shellhaven swung away and I looked down at the waters creaming way from our slewing hull. A red ensign stood out straighter from our sternpost.

At midday we dropped anchor off Southend amidst a multitude of naval and merchant ships of varied tonnage, type and nationality. An RAF fighter patrol left contrails high overhead. Shoals of basking barrage balloons glinted silvery over the Thames Valley. We lay there for three days. All requests for shore leave were denied, which always creates bad feeling, but it was a necessary evil since we would have to depart at short notice.

I was learning that monotony was the seafarer's worst enemy, especially when my companions had too much time on their hands. Being the newcomer, I was made the butt of time-honoured jokes. I was asked to shin up to the crow's nest to bring down eggs, and to ask Chippy for rubber nails and a left-handed screwdriver. As an evening mist spread across the estuary Roy asked me to get some fog blankets from the chief steward. I fell for one trick when, given a pair of binoculars by the bosun and asked to look at a particular point, I did so. The result was two black eyes from shoe-polished eye pieces. My last fool's errand was when the mate asked me to go down to the engine room for a bucket of steam. I returned with a bucket of water, explaining that the steam had condensed on the journey. He laughed heartily.

I enjoyed walking round the ship and making new acquaintances. Several had already experienced the terrors of being torpedoed, mined and bombed. One such was Alf Jones, an elderly greaser who came from Dalston, barely a ten-minute walk from my own home. He was frail, pallid and stooped, as if the machinery he tended had sucked out all his vitality. He had just had his second survivor's leave, having been on an iron ore ship coming home in convoy from Halifax when it was torpedoed just south of Ireland. Fortunately he was off-watch when the torpedo struck and wiped out all the engine room staff. By the time he got on deck the water was up to his thighs, and as he and another seaman made their way to the starboard lifeboat the deck fell away beneath them. His next recollection was coming to on a raft manned by four surviving shipmates. They gave him brandy and wrapped a duffel coat around his uncontrollably shivering body, holding and slapping him to keep him warm. Five hours later they were picked up by a destroyer. I asked Jones whether he had had enough.

'Too much. But it's my job. What other work could I do? I want to do my bit for the war effort.' He said it without affectation. He just meant it.

Later, when we had put to sea, Jones took me down below to show me what Dai called 'Dante's-Inferno-and-Hell rolled into one'. To me it was an awesome place. As I followed Jones onto the top level of steel grating I was hit by the heat, and I broke into an immediate sweat. It grew more intense as we travelled down from one level to the next, grimly clutching the slippery steel handrails, silvery through too much polishing. At last we reached the steel deck and I was mesmerised by the massive piston rods, behind which twisted and turned a jungle of lagged pipes of varying diameter. Massive steel tumblers thrashed around, turning the propeller shaft. The Danish fourth engineer called out a friendly greeting. He wore stained white dungarees and his men worked in singlets and shorts. All seemed to be in perpetual motion with their oil cans, balls of cotton waste and rags. Jones pointed to the catwalk way overhead.

'That's the waterline. When we're loaded it's much higher.' I imagined fractured pipes jetting out high-pressured scalding steam across the escape routes and water rushing in through a torpedo hole. I said I would not like his job. Jones smiled. 'You're not so well off either. When we're loaded you'll be sleeping six feet above the petrol cargo with only your deck in between.'

4

GOING TO SEA

It was a glorious day. Grey-white clouds sailed across the blue
skies and there was a gentle off-shore wind as our convoy made its
way around the coast. I was finally at sea. The *Venetia* developed
a steady roll. There was a tubby Belgian vessel on our port beam
and our North Sea side was guarded by two naval trawlers. A string
of flags was broken out on the commodore ship's halyards and was
immediately copied by other ships. The message read 'Enemy E-boats
are active in area. Outside ships must keep a sharp lookout.'

We passed the remains of ships that had been sunk by enemy
action. Mast tops protruded above the water singly, in pairs and
sometimes accompanied by the tops of funnels. Some exposed
their superstructure. One, which had turned turtle, to show its
entire barnacled stern, was graphically compared by Stevey to a fat
woman's bottom sticking out of Bournemouth's sands. A southbound
coaster limped by to seaward. Its boat-deck and bridge were riddled
and savaged. Her port lifeboat dangled from a single davit and men
were busily hauling it up. Her ensign flew at half mast and one of our
trawlers closed her. They exchanged aldis lamp signals.

They came out of the sun, three of them. Every ship seemed to
spot them at the same time. Sirens screamed out the short emergency

blasts. Guns started to chatter and bark. Smoke trails tangled and fiery balls rose to meet the diving German planes. I clutched the rail, fascinated, unable to move, watching one of the escorts hurling tracer at the aircraft. They approached with alarming speed. Our twin Lewis guns opened fire and I saw the marine sergeant behind them. Cartridge cases clattered onto the well-deck. The planes were running the length of the convoy, firing their guns and dropping bombs. Water spouts erupted between ships. For a moment their cross shapes projected shadows on the water. One explosion sounded different, metallic, rending. A tanker at the front end of the inside column stopped, black smoke rose from its foredeck and mushroomed skywards. As the *Venetia* swung out to give it a wide berth I could see its crew clustered around the perimeter of the damage. We moved back into line and very soon the incident might never have happened.

Back in my cabin I found a lifejacket had been placed on my bunk. It comprised two large cubes of canvassed cork, designed to be slipped over the head. Strings attached to the bottoms of the cubes had to be tied to hold it in place. The wearer, if forced to jump in the sea, was instructed to hold down the front cube with both hands, otherwise it would rise on impact and break his neck. It was known as the neck-breaker.

Smith came in and took me to task for having my cabin door shut.

'If we get hit and that door jams you'll never get out.' He pointed to the solid five-inch long brass hook at the top of the door and added, 'put that into the brass cleat and leave it there from now onward, all the time. You'll be on watch in five minutes. From now on we'll be on continuous watch, four hours on, four hours off, every day. For the watches we'll keep ship's time. We'll stick to Greenwich Mean Time for the log book entries. The radio cabin's chronometer is on Greenwich, while your wristwatch should show ship's time. You can decode incoming calls?' I nodded. 'Don't forget the drill on the bag.' This was a canvas bag heavily weighted with a lead bar. In the unlikely event of the *Venetia* being captured we had to put the log and coding and decoding books into it and drop it overboard.

'What about lunch?' I asked.

'I'll speak to Stevey about it,' said Smith. 'Sandwiches, not ham, not bacon, and duff with custard on top.'

Stevey brought me cheese sandwiches, which I was allergic to. I nibbled the bread, ate the duff and threw the cheese to the seagulls. Smith gave me the neck-breaker and said that henceforth I must always have it with me. Out on deck I breathed in the invigorating air. I was hungry but felt tremendously fit. Several ships were flying flimsy box kites, trailing wires. These were meant to entangle and bring down enemy aircraft, but were a joke weapon. Merchant seamen were not kite-flying enthusiasts.

The radio cabin was twelve feet by eight feet, and eight feet high. A flat-top desk occupied a third of its area. It supported the receiver, the transmission key and a row of meters. It also held the auto-alarm, a gadget designed to keep watch on the 600-metre wavelength. When it picked up a distress call it activated a loud alarm which before my arrival would bring Smith running from his bunk. My presence meant it was not needed, and Smith could have his rest. The bulkheads supported kilocycle tables, a radio map of the world and traffic schedules. I settled down into the comfortable swivel chair, threw in the high and low tension batteries and tuned into the 800-metre wavelength watch. My watches were 0400 hours to 0800 hours, 1200 hours to 1600 hours and 2000 hours to 2400 hours. Smith took the intervening hours.

Everything in the cabin pulsated in sympathy with the *Venetia*'s engines. The steam radiator sizzled and leaked. The cabin became unbearably stuffy. The deckhead ventilator, which protruded onto the upper bridge, brought the occasional reassuring sound of voices. I had nearly dozed off when the telephone startled me, and I grabbed a pencil and recorded the message in the log, repeated over and over again.

'Blue blue blue de GNI GNI GNI ...' I blew up the voice tube connecting the radio cabin to the wheelhouse. Ian answered.

'Niton sending out blues.'

Very soon the other coastal stations were doing the same, warning of enemy aircraft crossing the English coast at various points. I religiously reported each one until Ian told me to report only those close to our position.

'What is our position?'

'Don't bother about it on coastal runs. When we get out to deep sea you'll have it every hour.'

Smith relieved me without a word of exchange, which was his usual way. I was enjoying the fresh air on the port side, watching the inviting haze of coast, when Johnny led me over to the starboard side to watch a destroyer, which was limping homewards like a lame dog. Her bows rose high and her mangled stern shipped water. A plane suddenly roared over the convoy. Ships opened fire.

'Bloody fools,' said Johnny equably. 'One of ours.'

'Is this really such a bad ship?' I asked.

'Oh, aye. Just look at the lousy food we're all getting. Can't help the old girl's age but there's no reason for the skimping on the food we all get.'

'Well its wartime and servicemen can't complain.'

'But we're civilians, Sparky. A postman carries on posting. A butcher sells his meat and a merchant seaman plies his trade.'

'Being a merchant seaman is more dangerous than being a postman or a butcher.'

'Aye.' Johnny patted my shoulder. 'It just shows that we both chose the wrong trade.'

I turned in and fell into an immediate sleep. Four hours passed too quickly. Before going back on watch I leant over the side, noting that the Belgian vessel was still abeam. Voices from the focsle were raised in argument as I entered the radio cabin, only the find the cockroaches out in force. I took to catapulting elastic bands at them, and actually scored a few hits, requiring me to wipe up the mess with scrap paper. I noted occasional signals in the log book and then, suddenly, I was electrified.

Within five minutes two distress calls came in from British merchantmen torpedoed to the north of Cape Wrath. Both vessels reported sinking fast and the abandoning of ships. The four S calls galvanised me. The SSSS, transmitted three times, was followed by the call signs of the stricken ship three times. Then followed precise longitude and latitude, three times, and other relevant details – weather and casualties. The call sign was important, as it allowed me to find the name of the ship in the call sign book. The letter 'G' prefixed all British call signs. RRRR denoted the ship was being attacked by a surface raider, MMMM meant hitting a mine, 'Blues' meant attack by enemy aircraft. I was so excited I rushed the messages to the mate, who was on watch. He showed little interest.

'Thanks, Sparky. We'll get many more before we get home.' He looked past me and was silent. I turned to find a very annoyed Mr Michaels. He wore a belted grey woollen dressing gown over read and black striped pyjamas. These were tucked into knee-high woollen stockings which disappeared into fur-lined suede slippers. The helmsman, all ears, concentrated on the wheel.

You are on watch?' Mr Michaels growled at me with unmistakable displeasure.

'Yessir. I took two distress messages and brought them up here.'

'Does the voice tube not work, sir?' Oh God, I had forgotten clean about it. I was at a loss for an excuse. What now? Mr Michaels spoke with great deliberation. 'In future, boy, do not leave your watch. Never. Understand?'

'Yes …' Mr Michaels' gimlet eyes cleared my confusion. I said very firmly, 'yes, sir.'

Feeling humiliated I slunk back to the radio cabin. Five minutes later the mate blew down the tube and chuckled,

'Put it behind you, lad. But, do use your voice tube. That's what it's there for.'

When Smith relieved me, as fresh and immaculate as ever in a clean shirt and knife-edged trousers, I confessed my gaffe. He was not pleased, not at all. I turned in, but just as I had drifted off Stevey woke me and told me to get dressed. I cocked an ear and noticed that the engines were stilled, no bells, no shouts, no whistles, and the talk coming up through the ventilator was strangely muffled.

'What's up?'

'We've run into a thick mist and tangled with a southbound convoy. There was a whale of a collision and all ships have dropped hooks until we can see. Ships can swing and drag anchors so the Old Man has put lookouts all round the ship.'

'Collision?'

'One of ours and one of theirs, I suppose. What a feast we'd make for the E-boats.'

It occurred to me that some poor devils might have been asleep, like I was, and been killed in their bunks. Stevey was more concerned with mundane matters, such as why every conceivable thing turned up to impede a voyage when he was on a scuttlebutt like the *Venetia*.

'Unable to get back to sleep, I read a book by a shaded light and was out on deck ten minutes before I was due to go on watch. The rising sun was dissolving the mist. Large masses became visible, taking firmer shape and hardening into detail – ships, cautiously sorting themselves back into their respective positions. All the northbound vessels except one took their stations. Three grubby coasters fighting for the same inside column station ignored apoplectic flag and aldis signals from the naval escort. These were perverse master mariners who took great delight in upsetting naval upstarts who told them what to do.

The galley wireless (all gossip was brought to and dispersed in the galley, often by Stevey) spread the word that the two ships which had collided had been taken to Hull. At breakfast, after my 0400 to 0800 hours watch, I commented on the fog to Johnny.

'Fog, Sparky!' interrupted Stevey. 'You call that a fog? It was a mere discolouration of the atmosphere! Four years ago when I was on a real ship, not like this one, we ran into a pea-souper off the Newfoundland banks. It was so dense you could have grabbed it in handfuls. It lasted for four days and nights, and if you lit a candle and held it an inch from your nose you couldn't see the flame. But I remember once, I was on the *Victoria Belle*. We were one day out of Vancouver bound for Yokohama ...'

Johnny and I sneaked away to his cabin. Johnny commented that when Stevey was in full flight he really believed what he was saying. He was a master at self deception.

'I know what you mean,' I said. 'The knack of eating the *Venetia*'s food lies exactly in that. I don't look at it. I imagine it is what it isn't, and I actually eat it.'

'That's not self deception,' corrected Johnny. 'That's hunger.'

5

ROUND THE COAST

Mr Michaels seldom came down to eat in the saloon, choosing instead to eat, sleep, work and read voraciously in his quarters. He had an extensive collection of books, but more intriguing were the half-inch thick pads of lined foolscap paper Stevey would sometimes see him writing in. They roused robust speculation. Were they his memoirs? Another Joseph Conrad? Certainly not a Jerome K. Jerome, mused the mate, humour and lightness of touch were not his style. He rarely strayed beyond his room, the chart room, the wheelhouse and the bridge.

Coming off the 0400 to 0800 hours watch I would go straight into breakfast and join Roy and Johnny. With Stevey we would banter happily; we had melded into a very comfortable foursome. Roy and Johnny would ceremoniously share my bacon and sausage, assuring me that their only concern was to keep me on the straight and narrow of my religion. Sometimes when we had strung out the meal too long we would hear the chief steward, Twitch, berating Stevey for letting us linger, but he refused to budge us. He was aware how much we needed to relax after keeping watch, and the saloon was an oasis of warmth and companionship. One morning Roy suggested that Stevey tell the steward to go about his business, leaving Stevey to lock the pantry, thus making our lingering presence less of a bother.

'Can't,' explained Stevey. 'I haven't got a key.'

'What?' We were all genuinely surprised at this.

'He's suspicious and secretive, more than anyone I've ever met. If I need something for Mr Michaels he opens up for me, stays till I've taken what I need, and locks up after me. And he's not generous. Maltese Johnny, the cook, was taking stick from the seamen and asked Twitch to increase rations. He was scolded for making trouble, and is now dead scared of him.'

Like a mechanical serpent the convoy skirted the contour of the coast, avoiding minefields, slipping through buoy lanes, edging round wrecks. Ships branched off into east coast ports. Others came out to join us. We passed a large southward-bound convoy to seaward of us. They were low in the water with cargo and some had large crates lashed to their decks. Two tankers flew the dangerous-cargo red B flag. The bosun explained.

'High octane tankers and ammunition and explosive carriers all fly the B flag when loaded. We will, on the way home, and be as welcome to our neighbours as mumps in a nursery.'

Every few hours a solitary Anson soared overhead, reassuring those on shore that we were still alive and steaming. Three unidentifiable planes high up, darting in and out of clouds, drove every ship to emergency stations. We picked up blues from shore stations with uncomfortable frequency and wondered which towns the Luftwaffe had targeted. Smith picked up four more SSSS calls from torpedoed merchantmen. I picked up two. Wrecks shimmered in the distance, then hung abeam and fell away astern. We passed the green-slimed hull of a ship breaking the surface like the blunt head of a sea monster. She was upright, as if her bows were buried in North Sea mud.

A spring cleaning bug blew up as suddenly as a squall and swept through the ship. I was sparked off when Mr Michaels appeared in the pantry unexpectedly and caught the chief steward wiping crockery with a filthy cloth. The former snatched it and dangled it at arm's length with the air of a medieval doctor forced to come in contact with the plague.

'Look at it! It's foul, filthy, stinking, putrescent, revolting. And the water in the sink. Black, scummy, greasy. The pantry smells, it's mucky, a sewer...'

'Aye, sir,' Twitch sounded hoarse. 'We'll do it right away.'

'We?' Mr Michaels glared at him. 'We ...?'

'Stevey, my assistant, and I ...'

'Certainly not. Your assistant is attending my quarters. You, sir, will do it yourself. And right away.'

And he did. The entire ship's company swept into an orgy of cleaning. Cabins were ripped apart, mattresses, bed linen, carpets and furnishings were washed and spread out on deck to dry. Nooks and crannies swam with disinfectant, and wood blocks spiked with nails filed to needle points and with poisoned tips were wedged into rat holes. The engineers destroyed their local insect life with an ingeniously contrived steam jet. Johnny and I worked as a team cleaning our cabins, and he laughed as I lifted my mattress and recoiled at the swarming cockroaches beneath.

'God, where do they come from?' Stevey came in and grinned.

'They have a fantastic sex life, Sparky. And you eat them.' I thought of the bread I ate every day, embedded with tiny pieces of insect like caraway seeds. 'The warmth of the galley attracts them, and they fall in the soup and get stuck in every dish Maltese Johnny makes.'

'Doesn't he fish them out?'

'If he did that, he'd have no time left for cooking.'

'Urgh. Go away!' Stevey chuckled and left.

That night, during my 2000 to 2400 hours watch, I fell foul of Mr Michaels twice, which highly displeased Smith when I told him. It was one of those odd nights when the Old Man did not sleep, instead wandering here and there with the aimlessness of an insomniac. Our first encounter was mid-watch when the monkey-island lookout brought me a mug of cocoa and two slices of toast. He opened the radio cabin door without knocking, and as a result I did not have time to pull the blackout curtain across the opening in time. A beam of light from the charging lamps and the desk lamp flashed out across the ship, and realising what was coming, the lookout fled, while I sat in trepidation. Mr Michaels came in and blasted me for having the displayed light and for having the door shut; it should have been on the hook with the gap covered by the cloth. Within a few minutes the mate voice-tubed me and said,

'Laddie, your ventilator is showing light. The captain's furious. Expect another visit.'

Somehow in all the kerfuffle, I had managed to knock awry the cover which could be slid across the bottom of the ventilator. I rectified the error and sat waiting for another verbal pasting, but Mr Michaels did not appear. It was a nerve-racking watch, but no more was heard about my carelessness. At 2245 GMT I logged an SSSS call from a British merchantman some hundred miles north-east of Peterhead.

When I came off watch the skies were clear and full of stars. The moon was very bright and I saw Bass Rock slide by. The other convoy ships made clear silhouettes. The mate joined me, puffing contentedly on his pipe. A greaser, oily and sweat-dried, clad only in a singlet and dungarees, stumbled along the flybridge bound for a shower and his bunk. He was black from head to toe.

The mate had just bid me goodnight when one of the leading ships hit a mine. We saw the flame flare to mast-top height, and then heard the explosion. The blast plucked at our clothes, and the whole convoy roused. Sirens played the emergency short blasts, guns were manned and boat crews stood by. Nothing galvanises the sleeping, the lethargic and the fatigued like those short burst alarms. Like magic the *Venetia*'s crew were on deck, clutching their neck-breakers and peering bemusedly out to sea as they speculated as to the cause of the explosion. Pyjamas peeped through the necks of sweaters and from under raincoats. Those not on duty took up their stations by the two lifeboats, one to port and the other to starboard at lower bridge level. The mate had moved up to a wing of the upper bridge, where he was talking with Mr Michaels.

We passed the sinking ship, a well-worn old tramp steamer. The captain and the mate doffed their caps. Some of the older men bowed their heads out of respect for those who must have surely died. The vessel was heeling over, her deck dipping below the water's surface. I watched a lifeboat, packed with survivors, pulling away from her. The mate came down and told everyone to quit their boat stations and go back to their bunks.

The next morning we anchored off Methil, in Fife. We were there for a week, but only Mr Michaels went ashore, and he on company business. No crew member was given shore leave, which was greatly frustrating for a group of healthy young men, thirsty and in sight of pubs, hungry and within a stone's throw of well-cooked meals, and seeing pretty girls through binoculars and unable to make their acquaintance. It was especially hard on Johnny, being so close to home and his mother but unable to see her. The mate, Roy, the bosun and others tried to jolly him out of his funk, and their compassion was admirable. The bosun said Johnny would be better once the *Venetia* was underway again, and he was right, but it took time.

The jaws of the Firth of Forth enclosed a busy sea terminus, and ships were continually arriving and departing. Groups of ships which had crossed the Atlantic safely with their cargos came in and joined two large southbound convoys. Others, in ballast, came in and rested, before once again running the gauntlet of U-boat alley. I saw the ships of our allies, Danes, Dutchmen, Norwegians, Belgians, Frenchmen, Poles and Greeks. There were neutrals with huge national flags painted on both their sides. The Swedes and especially the Finns were distrusted. British ships predominated.

'No wonder you Poms copped the world,' observed Roy provocatively. 'Your cockroach-carriers find their way everywhere.'

'Not to Australia if they can help it,' replied Stevey.

'If this wreck finds her way to Sydney harbour she'll have to find another second mate. I'll be off like a shot.'

'Let's hope we get there then.' Stevey always seemed to have the last word. He was much sharper than he pretended to be.

The first mate perceived that idleness and festering resentment over food could lead to trouble. He and the bosun had all the hands over the sides in stages, red-leading and painting, the sort of work that can always be found on any ship. A customs officer came aboard and sealed the radio cabin, overriding Smith's angry protests. With time to fill I jumped at Smith's directive to put up a new emergency aerial, persuaded the marine sergeant to show me how to dismantle and reassemble the twin Lewis guns, and had Johnny instruct me in the use of a sextant. Poor Johnny. He made depressing company and he knew it. The mate had asked Mr Michaels to give him two days ashore, but in vain. It was wartime, and orders to sail quickly could come anytime. It had happened that seamen ashore had missed sailings, leaving ships short-handed for the vital Atlantic crossing. No crew member of a ship in a convoy assembly port could go ashore.

But the waiting at Methil, after the waiting off Southend and in the Thames, was making the crew restless. They complained about the Old Man, the mates, the chief steward, the ship owners, the union of officials, their lack of privacy and, above all, the food. Johnny vouchsafed;

'There'll be trouble if we don't get a move on. Last night three seamen and a greaser tried to bribe a fishing boat to take them ashore. Fortunately, he was wise enough to refuse.'

On one of the few occasions when Mr Michaels joined us for a meal, an incident blew up. It was lunch, and tipped off to the captain's presence by Stevey, we wore our blues. The soup was unusually thin, putting me in mind of the old music hall joke about Blackpool landladies making turnip soup by waving a turnip over boiling water. Only Mr Michaels ate it, with noisy relish. Then, he looked around the table and asked,

'No appetites, gentlemen?'

The jest was not appreciated. Again, he was the only one who, together with Smith – he ate anything – tackled the wizened sausages and greasy boiled potatoes sitting in a revolting yellowish pool that must have been ancient margarine. We were not yet despairing, as if there was one stomach-filler we all banked on it was our pudding smothered in custard. Stevey, sensing the atmosphere, put down our dessert with all the gentleness of a blaster dealing with temperamental dynamite. We looked at our plates. Without doubt, the mate, Johnny and I would have just left the table without protest, but no such diffidence shackled Australian Roy. He leant back and yelled for the steward. Stevey shuffled back into the room, his face concerned.

Not you,' snapped Roy. 'I want the organ grinder responsible for this … this muck!'

Stevey grinned with relief and hurried out. Mr Michaels had been regarding Roy with an impassive stare.

'You are dissatisfied, Mr Garrett?' he said quietly.

'Too true, sir,' replied Roy bluntly.

The captain leaned back, his face expressionless, his eyes fixed on the portraits of Their Majesties. The mate was making a meal of tamping fresh tobacco into his pipe. Smith, Johnny and I stayed put. We wanted to be elsewhere, but it was understood that when Mr Michaels dined with us we could only vacate the table after him, unless permission was asked of and granted.

The chief steward sidled in. He had hastily donned a white jacket, but he was unshaved and his flannel trousers were stained. Roy waded into the attack.

'You're as scruffy and unappetising as your food.' Twitch bridled.

'I haven't come in here to be insulted.'

'I haven't started yet,' Roy tapped the plate before him. 'What do you call this?'

'Plum duff.' The steward's voice was like gravel being swirled around a tin. His nervous tic twitched his mouth in such a comical manner that I had an almost uncontrollable urge to giggle. I clenched my fingernails into my palms and bit my lip.

'Plum duff?'

'I said so, didn't I?'

'So you did.' Roy stood up and took his duff across to Twitch, thrusting it into his hands. 'Take it. Find me a plum, even a fraction of a plum. You'll need an ice pick to break through to its centre.' Roy returned to his seat, leaving the chief steward staring at the duff. Smith caught my eye and frowned, his way of telling to keep a low profile. Then, Mr Michaels intervened.

'It's edible, Mr Garrett. I have eaten mine.'

'No one else has, and you have no right to intervene.'

'No?' The Old Man put me in mind of a bird of prey, sure of its unassailability over lesser breeds. The chief steward wilted with relief. 'The food is fine. Men going to sea nowadays are namby-pamby.' Roy sighed with vexation and declared;

'Well, I wouldn't give this swill to a piggery!' Then, with great deliberation, he counter-punched. 'It is appalling that certain people line their pockets at the expense of a ship's company which deserves better ...' Twitch stopped looking relieved and his tic worked overtime.

'What are you insinuating, Mr Garrett?' Mr Michaels asked.

'I'm not insinuating. I'm telling it as it really is.' Roy then breached etiquette by striding from the saloon. The chief steward muttered something and made his escape.

'Insolent young puppy,' growled the captain. He turned to the mate. 'Well, Mr Parkinson, what comments do you have to make?'

'Simply this,' replied the mate. 'Tackle the source of the trouble, the chief steward. Now sir, have I your permission to leave the saloon?' Mr Michaels nodded. The mate left, followed shortly by the captain.

Later that day a shaven chief steward in a spotless white jacket paid a visit to the captain's quarters. The food improved immeasurably. For a while.

The very next day Mr Michaels went ashore to attend a convoy conference. Soon after his return the *Venetia* sailed, once a customs official had come aboard and unsealed the radio cabin. I asked him why it had had to be sealed in the first place, but he replied that he honestly didn't know and was just obeying orders. Everyone was happy to be on the move again, although the weather had turned raw and gloomy, with non-stop drizzle.

I watched other ships moving out to sea, knowing they would be our convoy companions. They comprised the usual mixed bag; smutty colliers, scavenging tramps, tankers, cargo-passengers and one high-profile luxury liner. The bosun jerked a thumb at it and remarked that she would stay with us until we hit the broad Atlantic, and then shoot off independently. She had the speed. Every ship flew its position pennants, and naval and civilian launches flitted perilously between the moving ships, loud-hailing last-minute messages. One chugged alongside the *Venetia*'s lowered gangway, trying without success to attract the attention of the bridge, then fell away.

'Couldn't have been important,' remarked Johnny. 'Probably the Old Man ducking a bill.'

In wider waters the convoy formed station, keeping the regulation two cables length between vessels. The cold wind was increasing towards gale force, and the seas had become very choppy. The *Venetia* was number 41, indicating she was the first ship in the fourth column. It was point position on an outside column. With the minimum of fuss the merchantmen moved into their positions, gently rolling with engines just turning over, waiting for the start. The commodore ship raised a flag to the top of its halyards and the oblong of ships lurched forward on the roughening green sea. Smoke trails thickened and weaved black skeins overhead, and some 1,500 Merchant Navy men on twenty-four ships gazed wistfully shorewards. All knew that some of them would never see home again.

'Hoist!' yelled Collins, the Cockney lookout on monkey-island. The next level down Johnny raised his binoculars to recognise the flags and shouted,

'K 7.' This meant that seven knots was the convoy speed.

Two armed trawlers, a sloop and a destroyer guarded our seaward and rear sides. A Lysander made lazy wide circles overhead. Every ship supported its clusters of swooping gulls as they fought over the food scraps flung to them by wasteful cooks and fastidious seamen. We passed buoys marking wrecks, sighted a battered stationary ship coastside, and steamed through a thick patch of debris – chairs, tea chests, planks and a damaged raft. The bosun said it was a pity to leave such good salvage. We saw a tug towing a stern-down freighter southwards, like an ant dragging a beetle.

The commodore ship flagged the convoy to close formation and increase lookouts after dark. We felt a little vulnerable in our point position. E-boats were active along this stretch of water and they were fast and packed a powerful punch.

The *Venetia*'s company fell into its sea routine with each man playing his essential role. The three mates maintained a continuous bridge watch. Third mate Ian was signals officer, second mate Roy was chart and timekeeper and the first mate oversaw the general handling of the deck side of the ship. All three mates could handle all the jobs. Johnny was dogsbody, and was called upon to tackle anything that needed doing; he was learning all the time.

The deck officers worked through the bosun and it was he who kept the seamen maintaining, repairing and generally seeing that everything worked smoothly. The carpenter, Chippy, sounded bilges, oiled and renovated any woodwork that required attention. His workshop was larger than his cabin, such was his workload, and there was always more wood in his cabin than in his workshop. He gave all the sawdust to Maltese Johnny for the floor of his galley.

Chippy was a tall, white-haired man from Middlesbrough, and when not working for the ship he carved the most lifelike animals from wood. If you half-closed your eyes and stared at them they seemed to move. A lot of the small tools fastened into ingenious racks on the walls were of his own invention. He explained to Ernie Charlton, the second engineer, what he wanted, and Ernie would make the tool for him. Chippy had a large collection of books and magazines that covered every animal you could think of. His long, calloused fingers showed an amazing delicacy of touch as he varnished and painted his models. He gave me a nine-inch model of a porcupine, the spines in wood, as delicate as filigree work. He carefully packed his models into a tea chest, and when we reached a home port he would send them home to his wife in Northumbria, who would sell them to shops and stores. When he explained the different qualities of wood his face would light up. His favourite was the slowest growing of trees, the walnut.

As the convoy crept northwards into more open waters the weather became more bleak. The temperature dropped sharply, and increasing winds whipped creamy spindrift across the chasing waves. We ploughed through belts of rain. Johnny gave me a balaclava, which I found unbearably itchy at first, then useful, and as the weather worsened, indispensible. A severe cold had my eyes and nose streaming and affected my watch-keeping. Smith berated me mercilessly for being careless enough to come down with such an avoidable indisposition. He ordered me to see Mr Michaels. He added that if I went down with a cold he would be very displeased with me. I could have guessed that.

It was with the utmost trepidation that I knocked at the door of the captain's quarters. He expressed such glee that I felt more like a victim than a patient. We went downstairs to the dispensary adjoining the pantry, and he carefully selected a large beaker, washed it out and poured equal quantities from seven different bottles into it. All the time he hummed and stirred, and the mixture changed colour with each addition from colourless to a dark brown. I ventured that I was feeling much better and drier. Even if that had been the case, said Mr Michaels firmly, the concoction was too good to waste. He gave it a final vigorous stir and handed it to me.

'Does it need water, sir?'

'What? Dilute it with water? Are you off your head, boy? Get it down.'

I drank. Molten steel seemed to burn my throat. I gasped and choked and thought of homicidal mariners and sulphuric acid. I broke out into an instantaneous sweat, my windpipe expanded and phlegm retreated. My sinuses dried up and my head began to swim. Stevey appeared at the door just as I began to doubt my ability to stand steady. The Old Man summed me up and said;

'Sit you down for a wee while, boy.' He gave Stevey the key to the dispensary and told him to bring it up to him once I was recovered enough to move. Once he was gone I glowered at the amused Stevey.

'What happens if I get appendicitis?'

'Better keep quiet about it. He's got a medicine chest with the most wicked collection of scalpels I've ever seen.'

I kept my 2000 to 2400 hours watch. The radio cabin smelled strongly of Dettol disinfectant. Almost at once I picked up three SSSS calls from the west of Rockall, way out in the Atlantic. Reception was strong. Despite our four escorts we sensed the tautness of entering more dangerous waters. U-boat alley was beckoning.

After breakfast the next morning I was washing my underwear, handkerchiefs and constrictive white collars when the short blasts of the emergency siren had me grabbing my lifejacket and hurrying out on deck. I saw the denizens of the focsle running out onto the well-

Morris aged eighteen, a few months before joining the Merchant Navy. He stands with his cousin, Sam Rosenblatt, Hackney, 1939.

Wearing the 'blues' bought at Gardiners, the famous outfitters in Aldgate of the Royal and Merchant Navies.

Official certificate photograph, May 1940.

Out on deck in the sunny Carribean.

No. C/1966

UNITED KINGDOM OF GREAT BRITAIN AND NORTHERN IRELAND

Special Certificate of Proficiency in Radiotelegraphy granted by the Postmaster General for Radiotelegraph Operator on board a ship to which the Merchant Shipping (Wireless Telegraphy) Act, 1919, and the Merchant Shipping (Safety and Load Line Conventions) Act, 1932, do not apply.

This is to certify that under the provisions of the General Radiocommunication Regulations annexed to the International Telecommunication Convention, 1932, Mr. *Morris Beckman* has been examined in Radiotelegraphy and has passed in :—

(*a*) Elementary knowledge of the adjustment and practical working of apparatus.

(*b*) Sending, and receiving by ear, in the Morse Code, messages in plain language at a speed of not less than 20 words a minute, and in code groups at a speed of not less than 16 groups a minute.

(*c*) Knowledge of the regulations applying to the exchange of radio-communications, and of the part of the Radiocommunication Regulations relating to the safety of life.

(*d*) Sending and receiving spoken messages correctly by telephone.

It is also certified hereby that the holder has made a declaration that he will preserve the secrecy of correspondence.

Signature of examining officer *G.D. Henchman*

The holder of this special Certificate is hereby authorised to operate radiotelegraph and radiotelephone apparatus on board any British ship which is not compulsorily provided with a radio installation, but not on any ship within the scope of the Merchant Shipping (Wireless Telegraphy) Act, 1919, and the Merchant Shipping (Safety and Load Line Conventions) Act, 1932.

Y.G. Crocker for the Postmaster General, G.P.O., London.

24 JUN 1940 Date.

Signature of holder *M. Beckman*

Date of Birth *21st February 1921* Place of Birth *London*

The authority granted by this Certificate may be withdrawn by the Postmaster General at any time at his discretion. The holder of the Certificate shall return the Certificate to the Postmaster General upon receiving from him notice of the withdrawal of the authority granted thereby. Until so withdrawn the authority granted by the Certificate shall continue in force so long as the provisions of the International Telecommunication Convention concluded in Madrid in 1932 remain in force.

This Certificate should be carefully preserved. In case of loss through avoidable causes, a duplicate will only be issued on payment of a fee of not less than 10s.

Any person other than the owner thereof becoming possessed of this Certificate should send it forthwith to the Inspector of Wireless Telegraphy, General Post Office, London, E.C.1.

K 704

10/39—[12273] 11308 5/40 696

A radio officer hard at work on board a merchant vessel.

Beckman firing twin Lewis guns with a naval instructor standing by.

Two views of an Atlantic convoy. (Library of Congress)

British merchant vessel
sunk by a mine.

A torpedoed ship goes
down. This was the fate
of 108 British merchant
ships during the first five
months of 1940.

Below and below right:
Merchant seamen in
lifeboats following the
sinking of their ship.
(Author's photos)

Above: Krupp Germania Works in Kiel, where many Type VII U-boats were built before being sent out to hunt the Allied convoys.

Left: A U-boat captured by the Royal Navy.

Below left and right: Life on board a submarine.

British merchant seamen and US Rangers in a joint convoy. The US Liberty Ships and the entry of America into the war would eventually guarantee victory for the Allies in the Battle of the Atlantic. Such a victory looked a horribly long way off in 1940. (Library of Congress)

MERCHANT NAVY A/A GUNNERY COURSE.

CERTIFICATE OF PROFICIENCY

CANADA

D.E.M.S.
TRAINING CENTRE

AUG 8 19..

SYDNEY, CANADA

Date stamp of Training Centre

Name ...M. Beckman...

Rank or Rating... 2nd Radio Officer...

B. of T. or D.B No... S.S. Eversleigh...

has completed the Merchant Navy A/A Gunnery Course and is qualified in the firing, cleaning and lubrication ... 5 1 Oerlikon.. machine gun.

Rank... J. Bygden... Lt. R.C.N.V.R.

D.E.M.S.
Training Centre... Sydney N.S.

10M-5-42(M1081)

Certificate earned for completing a gunnery course in Canada. Beckman went on to complete two others in Bombay and England.

C.R.S. 8.
(Revised 10/42)

MERCHANT NAVY RESERVE POOL

Certificate of Discharge from Merchant Navy Service

This is to Certify that (full name)...........Morris BECKMAN

born on 21st February, 1921 at Hackney, London...........Dis. A. No. R207464

Rank or Rating........Radio Officer........is discharged from service in the Merchant Navy.

His National Service Acts Registration No. is MMB/21/134328........(to be completed in all appropriate cases).

The reason for his discharge is that he is........Ceasing to be fit for sea

Signature of Seaman: Morris Beckman

THIS FORM MUST BE CAREFULLY PRESERVED BY THE OFFICER OR RATING TO WHOM IT IS ISSUED. IT MUST NOT BE TRANSFERRED TO ANY OTHER PERSON.

OFFICE STAMP

The above has surrendered his British Seaman's Identity Card (Serial No. BS 56639) and forms C.R.S. 56 and 76 have been issued.

Superintendent and National Service Officer. and Assistant Registrar General.

28/4/45

To be prepared in triplicate.
Top copy to Seaman. Carbons to R. G. S. & S. and Reserve Pool Office concerned.

(3.807D) Wt 47911/311 150 Pads 1/45 H J R & L Gp 51

Morris Beckman in later years.

deck and our marines hurtled past on their way up to monkey-island. A German fighter-bomber was coming towards us. Streams of tracer from other ships converged on it, and our marines were firing the Lewis guns. It was like a dream. Two black specks detached from the aircraft's fuselage, its engines vibrating the air.

Wait for it. Wait for it. The convoy held its breath and then two columns of water leapt high between the second and third columns. Suddenly the plane jerked, faltered and appeared to lose speed and height. All guns stopped firing. I heard sporadic cheering from various ships, ours as well. Then, the plane recovered, picked up speed and hurtled away in the direction of France.

Later that day the lead ship in the second column struck a mine. The explosion broke her back; she settled fast on a weirdly even keel, as if a giant hand was pulling her downwards. She was gone quickly, leaving behind a boat cramped with men, wreckage and the less fortunate swimming in cold water. A naval trawler moved across to pick them up. The commodore ship instructed all others to maintain station as they were. That was war at sea for the sitting duck navy, just like that, sudden death without warning. Roy put his hand on my shoulder.

'Outward bound, in ballast, not so bad, Sparky. Homeward bound, loaded, we'll really have tankeritis.'

'What's that?'

'We'll do our job. We'll know our cargo and nothing can stop you thinking about it. That's tankeritis.'

On 9 August we passed by Kinneard Head. I was allowed free run on the upper bridge and spent much time staring coastwards through binoculars, a soothing pastime, even though the comforting Scottish coast to port was often hazed by mist and rainfall. We passed by Aberdeen, Peterhead and Frazer. They were too distant to be seen. Land fell astern out of sight and a long deep swell had the *Venetia* rolling as never before since we had left the Thames. All moveable, objects were fastened down and Stevey covered the saloon table with small wooden squares. They slotted into one another and were designed to stop what was on the table sliding to and fro. I suffered real seasickness and had to excuse myself from the breakfast table.

'Oh dear,' said Roy. 'Poor Sparky. I'll have to have his egg and you can have his baked beans.'

'That's not fair,' protested Johnny. 'We should toss for the egg.'

'I'm pulling rank, Johnny,' said Roy, and to the amusement of Stevey he forked my egg onto his plate. I managed to get onto the well-deck in time to throw up into the sea.

Rounding Pentland Firth, the north-easterly tip of Scotland that harbours John O'Groats, the convoy turned towards the west. One morning when I came off watch I saw that the liner had gone. Opinion had it that she was bound for Montreal to pick up Canadian troops. The two naval trawlers had also gone and that same afternoon the sloop bade us farewell and headed back when we had come. We all understood that the Royal Navy was very thinly stretched with all the ocean it had to cover, but nevertheless, with just one destroyer we felt more vulnerable than ever. The next day, to our great delight, another destroyer turned up. There was no happier sight to a merchant seaman than seeing destroyers sheep-dogging a convoy. I was so distracted by my joy that I incurred the displeasure of Smith by relieving him without having my neck-breaker to hand. He sent me back to my cabin to retrieve it and gave me a deserved dressing down.

Alert and as stealthy as a hunted animal we crept along, the convoy dependent on its radios for its sight and hearing. Its aerials were its antennae, warning it of approaching perils and giving it time to take evasive action. Smith and I kept permanent watch on the 600-metre wavelength.

The messages we looked for were the ones coming from the transmission station at Rugby, which were prefixed 'GBR' when they were for British ships. They came in code, and decoding always broke the monotony. Rugby was the most powerful transmitting station and it was said that its messages could reach ships in all the oceans and seas of the world. GBR messages from Rugby warned of U-boat and E-boat activity in certain areas, of danger from loose mines and instructed convoys to alter course to avoid specific hazards. There were occasional messages for individual ships. Constant practice on the dead key had improved my Morse transmission in speed and spacing no end.

Large coastal command flying boats sometimes circled us during the days. Some three hours across every dawn the mate increased our lookouts. During a 2400 to 0400 hours watch Ian reported gun flashes to the north, which lasted about five minutes. Our destroyer took up position between us and the flashes, but it dared not leave the convoy unprotected. We never learned what took place.

As we closed with the north-western approaches the feeling of impending battle manifested itself in a certain extra edginess. The gale force winds made keeping station difficult, yet every afternoon the destroyer would herd us closer together, supposedly to make it easier for it to protect us. Johnny would do his rounds checking blackout precautions and the Red Ensign would be hauled down.

With relentless regularity the distress calls came in. Two enemy planes left a British vessel sinking in the North Sea. A convoy, homeward bound from Halifax in Nova Scotia, lost four ships in ten minutes. The efficient Smith disentangled the distress calls, which were almost simultaneous. A Greek went down off the Faroes. The transmissions were frequently jerky and too fast, with no spacing between the words. The final call from a lone ship, perhaps a straggler left behind when her engines broke down, was the usual SSSS and ended with the words 'Going fast. Taking to boats. Terrible waves. Help.'

Roy's outburst in the saloon had improved the food so dramatically that we even had bowls of tinned peaches and pears. However, the quality was gradually waning. I was always hungry. Keeping watch is a sedentary occupation and I found it hard to sit for more than half an hour, and would walk in a tight semi-circle around the desk, attached to the receiver like a dog on a leash. Off watch I would visit Pablo Valdez and learn Spanish and play chess. I also spent time with Chippy. He was an easy man to be with and we would talk while he carved his animals. Once he gave me a block of wood and tried to teach me to make a dog. I was hopeless, but he was very patient.

Apart from the chief steward, who I did not like, I chatted with many of the crew. I found them friendly and always interesting, especially the older ones who seemed to have been in every port in the world. Some never got past the dockside and could well have written the definitive academic tome on the bars, brothels and clip joints of the seven seas. Others had surprising pastimes and hobbies. Arne Rolleson, a Dane, was the fourth engineer. He had worked on ocean-going cargo-passenger boats. He was in New York when the Germans invaded Denmark, and had made his way back to England to fight with the Free Danish Forces. His ship was torpedoed between Bermuda and the UK, and he had lost his beloved piano accordion, which he had played as a soloist with bands across Scandinavia. He decided not to buy another until the war ended. Once in England, to his chagrin, he was directed into the Merchant Navy, where he was told he would be of more use. He was Viking blonde, quiet, and according to others a first-class engineer.

Long John, so-called because he was six feet two inches tall, was an able seaman. He came from Stroud in Gloucestershire, and still had a West Country burr in his speech. His passion was ballroom dancing, and with his partner he had won prizes in competitions throughout the Midlands and West Country. When he was ashore he would go to London to meet his partner and visit West End dance halls with their big band music. He said that if he survived the war he would go in for it professionally. He was still young enough.

We rounded Cape Wrath and headed south into the North Minch. The gales blew themselves out and we had blue skies and sunshine. It was incredible how often and swiftly the weather changed. Outside the focsle washing lines appeared. I suddenly found my sea legs. It was a relief to not to have to think about where to tread. We steamed southwards into the Little Minch and the land looked inviting. Here another ship put up the two black balls indicating distress. Engine trouble. It fell back and a destroyer went after it, returning an hour later. The straggler never rejoined us. The bosun, the most dependable and best-liked man aboard, joined me on the port wing of the bridge.

'She's lucky. She'll be safe enough in the Minches. There's a tug on its way out to her now, I'll be bound. But, to straggle in the Atlantic …' he shook his head. 'That's like playing Russian roulette.'

He asked me how I had come to be in the Merchant Navy, and after I had told my story he told his. He came from Bristol, from a prosperous family. His father was an antique dealer and had two shops, and had paid for him to have a good education, hoping he would go into the family business. However, the perverse spirit of a piratical ancestor must have lurked in the bosun's blood, for after a horrendous quarrel with his father he had walked down to Avonmouth and signed on a tramp as a deckhand. It was away for two years, and in that time he visited the South Seas, the Far East and the Antipodes. He caught the seafaring bug. On his return his father told him that now he had seen the world he should come home and work, but after more rows the bosun returned to the sea for good. His younger brother took over the family business, which mollified his father. The bosun only bothered to go home when his ship berthed in a west coast port, and then only to see his mother.

Southwards through the Inner Hebrides and the Outer Hebrides. We passed through their two sentinel islands, Barra to our starboard and Tiree to our port, and altered course westwards. This area, north of Ireland, provided rich pickings for the U-boats, and the seasoned veterans amongst the crew enjoyed chilling the blood of newcomers like myself with tales of torpedoes.

I came off my late morning watch to find that a third of the convoy's ships had peeled away and left us, although we still had our destroyer escort. At breakfast, Johnny filled me in.

'Those ships are heading south through the Irish Sea to make for the Bay of Biscay and thence to Gibraltar, West Africa, South Africa and even round the Cape to India.'

'The English Channel is a shorter route, surely ...'

'Think, Sparky, think,' said Roy, as he speared my sausage onto his plate. 'To send a convoy across the Channel would be too dangerous and would take too many protective resources. The RAF and Royal Navy have to be miserly with what they've got at the moment. Imagine the air and sea losses to protect just one convoy.'

The convoy was down to sixteen ships. A Blue Star Line passenger-cargo ship became our new commodore vessel. Its first action was to increase speed to eight knots, a message we received at 1000 hours, ship's time. It was the mate's watch and the captain was with him when he rang the engine room for more revolutions to increase speed. Dai was on watch and shrilled his displeasure back through the voice tube;

'Can't do it.'

'Must have it,' said the mate equably.

'She's on blood as it is ...'

'It's the convoy speed, Dai.'

'Impossible.'

Mr Michaels tried to take the voice tube from the mate, but the latter gently but firmly resisted.

'Then do the impossible, Dai.'

'Alright, but when the boilers go through the skylight and us with them you'll be to blame.'

The mate smiled as he replaced the tube. Mr Michaels snorted.

'Bloody recalcitrant engineers.'

6

U-BOAT ALLEY

Our small convoy of sixteen ships closed in. There were four columns of four and we remained in point position, number forty-one. We steamed on a north-westerly course, and crossing to the west of longitude eight degrees we entered the Atlantic Ocean and U-boat alley. Our destroyer took up position at our rear. From now on the mood was one of alert expectancy. War at sea is sudden and violent. The danger from mines, E-boats and land-based air attacks was behind us. Now, our hunters were the giant Focke-Wulfs which ranged thousands of miles like huge birds of prey, giving extra pairs of eyes to the U-boats lurking beneath the waves.

The first night we were on our own we ran into solid cloud cover. The moon and stars vanished and the impenetrable darkness defeated the lookouts. A strong wind blew up and rain lashed across the *Venetia* as she bucked and rolled. The engineers down below balanced like ballet dancers as they slaved to keep the ship's revolutions up to the speed demanded. The greasers were stripped down to their underwear, streaming with sweat and with the agility of monkeys. They griped continually, which helped to push away their apprehensions, the main one being the fear of a torpedo striking the engine room. To them, the ship was too light in ballast, her screw lifted too often out of the water, she had been

71

laid up too long, her bottom needed scraping and the engines were clapped out.

Day after day slipped by in an endless succession of watches on and watches off as we edged in a north-westerly direction across the Atlantic. Squalls and gales alternated with periods of calm. I lost my seasickness and at breakfast I was eating more of my bacon, urged on by Stevey who told me not to let 'the other two greedy bastards' get it. I read avidly whatever I could scrounge, and was delighted to come across a copy of *Ben Hur*. I had only got halfway through when it disappeared. The loss was blamed on the fourth mate, a useful fictitious character at whose door the blame was laid whenever anything went wrong or missing. I was not the only one who kept away the boredom with literature. Stevey was found reading the Old Testament, and when ribbed, blustered that it had some good yarns in it.

None to compare with some of yours,' laughed Roy.

On his 1600 to 2000 hours watch Smith logged a grain carrier in trouble. She sent out an ordinary SOS, and Smith commented that she was probably overloaded and that if the sea got into the cargo it would swell beyond control, the force of which could pop steel rivets and planking. It was not a cargo particularly liked by merchant seamen. He also logged two torpedoings well to the south. Within a minute of my relieving him I picked up an SSSS from a Britisher just thirty miles ahead. This close encounter galvanised the commodore into altering course almost due north. Our destroyer took up position on our port flank, between us and the reported attack. Once or twice it dropped a depth charge pattern and circled round the disturbance. A permanent air of menace persisted.

Yet, what really engaged the crew's attention and emotion was food. It had slumped right back to virtually inedible quality. Thanks to Roy's outburst the food in the saloon was still acceptable, and it was haute cuisine compared to what was dished out to the residents of the focsle. This made us all, except perhaps Mr Michaels, uncomfortable.

The seamen grumbled like lions and behaved like lambs, until, that is, the chief steward and able seaman Kenny exchanged words and then blows on the flybridge. Stevey rushed to prise them apart, which was fortunate for Twitch. The next day I was checking the specific gravities and liquid levels in the wet batteries on monkey-island when I heard shouting. I looked down and saw a knot of men clustered around the galley. They were shouting at the cook, Maltese Johnny, who was protesting that if the chief steward gave him better ingredients and more of them he could cook better meals. The bosun appeared and dispersed the angry seamen.

When I relieved Smith I told him what I had seen and that the seamen could not be blamed for raising the issue. Smith threw me the icy stare which I was getting to know and said that it was none of my business.

'I was expressing my opinion, that's all.'

'Well don't,' replied Smith. 'I really don't want to keep reminding you that our job is running an efficient radio department and that's it. I don't want you to get caught up in any troubles that do not concern us. Do I make myself clear?'

'Absolutely,' I nodded.

But a ship is a small place and the well-deck was the *Venetia*'s Piccadilly Circus. If you wanted a blow or a short stroll, that was where you went, and the next morning, after Roy, Johnny, Stevey and I had discussed the seamen's grievance and sided with them, for that was all we could do, I was out on deck for my usual walk. As I leaned on the rail watching the other ships, four men approached from the focsle. They were led by Wilkie, a tall, powerful Southern Irishman. We had conversed before and he seemed well educated and articulate, making me wonder at the time what on earth he was doing as an able seaman.

Wilkie looked confident, but his three companions did not. Two of them carried large trays which supported two mounds of herring charred into a congealed and inseparable mass. Wilkie leaned alongside me.

'Would you like to eat a forkful of that mess, Sparky?'

'Er, no thanks.' I prayed that Smith was glued to the desk of the radio cabin and not standing by the open door, as we both often did during daylight hours.

'Try it,' persisted Wilkie. I felt a touch of anger. I knew that there were always men on lookout or on the upper bridge at this time of day who would notice anything unusual, and sure enough I heard the unmistakeable voice of Mr Michaels.

'What damn nonsense is going on down there?'

Wilkie turned away from me and stared up at the Old Man. His three followers fidgeted uncomfortably, but not Wilkie. He just called them to follow him and strode to the companionway and ascended to the lower bridge deck to confront the captain. They straggled somewhat, and as if by magic, news of the coming clash spread around the ship. Men off watch suddenly appeared, Maltese Johnny emerged from his galley and lookouts surreptitiously ignored marine perils to concentrate on the excitement.

Wilkie and the captain stood face to face and the former held a tray under Mr Michaels' nose for inspection.

'Would you consider this a fit breakfast for six men who work hard and conscientiously in the most arduous of conditions, sir?'

'Aye. It's good nourishing protein, Mr Wilkie.'

'Then perhaps, sir, you would partake of this excellent nourishing protein.' Wilkie produced a fork from a pocket, dug into the mass of herring and proffered it to the captain. Watchers held their breath. It was an unexpected challenge. Mr Michaels was forced to resort to his one unassailable trump card, his authority. With a sweep of his arm he knocked the fork flying and ordered Wilkie to stand down off the lower bridge and depart. Wilkie stood his ground and said with deliberate civility:

'I have been appointed spokesman for the hands to request food that is fit to eat ... sir.' A contemptuous pause before the 'sir'. Mr Michaels raised his voice.

'I'm ordering you to get below, sir.' Wilkie made no move.

'I take it, sir, that you will improve our food forthwith,' he said politely. Maybe it was that peremptory 'forthwith' that enraged Mr Michaels more than the demand.

'I'll have no impertinent sea lawyer arguing with me, sir. Now get below!'

'Will you improve our food?'

'You are logged five shillings for insubordination.'

'What insubordination?'

'Not getting below when I ordered you to do so. For continuing to disobey I am logging you another two pounds, sir.'

Wilkie gave way, slowly. The captain's authority to punish made it no contest. He followed his comrades who were already back on the well-deck, then electrified everyone by hurling the trays of herrings into the sea and yelling back at the captain,

'If we don't eat properly we won't be able to work properly ... sir.'

'For wilful damage, sir, you are logged another ten shillings,' responded Mr Michaels, then disappeared into his quarters.

Stevey exhaled a long drawn out breath, and that said it all.

The chief engineer paid a rare visit to the captain's quarters. He was a stocky, grey-haired scot from Ayr in his fifties called Norman Mallinson. He kept himself to himself and rarely ventured outside his aft accommodation, the engine room and workshop. His whole world revolved around the engine and staff, and it needed no Sherlock Holmes to know why he paid the call. Wilkie had brought to the surface the underlying bitterness felt by the men over the food, and it could no longer be ignored by those responsible. The chief steward had always kept a low profile, but now he was out of sight. Stevey, the ship's verbal columnist, reported that for the first time Maltese

Johnny was being allowed to choose the ingredients he used. The food now showed its most marked improvement. It came out later that the mate had tried to persuade the captain to reduce Wilkie's fines, but he would have none of it. It was possibly the throwing of company property overboard that made the penalty irrevocable.

Later that same eventful day the convoy ran into another heavy blow. High combers raced across from horizon to horizon and the empty ships danced like agitated corks on the surface of a disturbed pond. Many made heavy going and in the late afternoon a British freighter put up the two black balls which denoted that she was without power. She fell astern of the convoy. The destroyer held a short exchange of aldis signals with her but did not dare leave the convoy unescorted, and the freighter did not rejoin us. Smith and I listened acutely for an SSSS call from her, but one never came.

The weather worsened and foamy walls of water stood on the *Venetia*'s stern and flipped her over onto her bows. Even the seasoned seamen, who could usually juggle balls on a bucking ship, had to consciously balance themselves. Mandel, a young Pole who had escaped the Nazi occupation of his country and reached England via the Romanian port of Constanza, was thrown from the gun-deck ladder and cracked his knee on an iron cleat. He was an ordinary seaman on his second voyage, spoke very little English and was rather introverted and broody, but he was quick to learn and a willing worker. He saw Mr Michaels, who dressed his wound and rebuked him for his carelessness, saying;

'It's work we want from you, young man, not injuries.'

Mandel limped for weeks afterwards, but he pulled his weight.

We were now well into U-boat alley. Did the Germans know of our existence? That was the topic of the moment, and the next evening we had our answer. A Greek vessel, a refugee from the Mediterranean trade, showed black balls and fell astern. Our destroyer exchanged aldis signals as usual, but we had to leave the stragglers. Before going on my 2000 to 2400 hours watch I was on deck. It was still light, with the first brushes of darkness creeping across the convoy, when I heard the explosion, muffled by distance. The *Venetia* rose on a crest and I glimpsed a tiny ball of flame and smoke far astern. I dashed into the radio cabin as Smith was logging the distress call.

'Our Greek?' he nodded. Our destroyer signalled for the convoy to close up and patrolled a line across the rear, backwards and forwards. There was little else she could do. I went back on deck and was met by the bosun.

'What about picking up survivors?' I asked him.

'What about it?' repeated the bosun. 'We can't. The escort can't desert fourteen of us for one ship. That bugger has been stalking us. Yep. Jerry certainly knows we exist and where we are.'

No one needed to be reminded to have their neck-breakers always to hand. The mate organised more lookouts. The marine sergeant organised a continuous gun watch incorporating his Merchant Navy volunteers. The captain warned Johnny:

'If here is so much as a pin of light it will be God help you and the idiot responsible.'

The commodore ship, after an exchange of aldis signals with the destroyer, ran up the last flag signal of the day. It read 'Expect attack. Close up. If attacked the convoy will immediately disperse. All ships will continue independently to destinations.'

By the time I went on watch Smith had collected two more SSSS calls just to the north-west of Ireland. Every thirty minutes the mate sent me down our precise latitude and longitude, and I practised sending out a mock SSSS distress call several times. Few of the crew slept well that night; we had been found. Even now U-boats could be converging to slaughter us, and those off watch lay in bed with lifejackets and shoes on. As for me, sitting in the radio cabin, I thought about our position at point on an outside column, as exposed as a coconut on a stick at a fair.

After my watch had ended I stood on the well-deck and enjoyed the new warmth that the air had, and looked at the enormous moon. The silhouettes of the other ships stood out boldly, making them look like excellent targets. Roy came down from the bridge.

'Do you play draughts, Sparky?'

'God, that's a funny question. I do play.'

'Sleepy?'

'Not at all.'

We sat at the saloon table and played draughts. Roy sipped brandy from a silver flask, then poured some in a tumbler for me. I declined, but he refused to take no for an answer. I drank gingerly, and the more I drank the better I liked it. Our ears strained for any sound out of the ordinary. It was a strange game.

'Just imagine,' Roy said, rather maudlin, 'right now, Sparky, a tinfish could be speeding towards us. It could come right through the plates and land here.' He banged the table between us. 'And then, what?'

'You and the other greedy sod would get no more of my sausage and bacon,' I said, and we both fell about laughing.

The expected attack did not materialise, but when day broke and the sun rose high no one was in a singing mood. We counted the ships, and apart from the straggler we had left behind in the Minches and the torpedoed Greek, no others were missing. I had cause to regret the brandy I had drunk, as on my 0400 to 0800 hours watch I had the devil of a time keeping awake. The warmth and stuffiness of the radio cabin made matters worse, and Smith had noted my lethargy when I had relieved him, pointedly sniffing and looking at me accusingly, but saying nothing. Straight after breakfast I turned in, and had just fallen asleep with all my clothes on when we ran into a sudden squall and I was woken by a tremendous crashing. Heart in mouth, I sat up, only to hear Stevey and the chief steward cursing the weather and each other for the demise of a carelessly stacked pile of crockery.

'There go some of your ill-gotten profits,' said Stevey.

'You'd better mind what you bloody well say,' warned Twitch.

So, it carried on. I fell asleep again. When the lookout shook me awake there were a pair of woollen sea stockings on my chest; inside one was a card decorated with flowers and birds and a message which read 'Dear boy, whoever you are, I hope you find these useful.' Johnny was luckier. In his pair of gloves he found a name and address, and said he would write back.

'Probably a seductive, one-eyed, one-legged nonagenarian,' I growled.

'Sour grapes, Sparky,' he laughed.

The squall blew itself out, leaving an angry ocean and sullen skies. But it left cold in its wake, and deck working parties wore gloves, jerseys and the odd balaclava. My cabin radiator packed up, but Harry Reed fixed it for me, blaming a malfunctioning valve.

'Bloody valves and bearings give us most of our troubles.'

All ships were on fullest alert. The destroyer patrolled the rear and flanks actively, but now that we had been found there was not a single man in the convoy that would have bet against us being attacked. When and by how many U-boats were the two questions. When I relieved Smith at noon he was unusually uncommunicative, and we made the change without a word passing between us. A message from GBR (Rugby) transmitting station to all British ships warned of German raiders loose in the mid-Atlantic. I notified Ian via the voice tube to the wheelhouse, whose response was 'Oh really?'

I turned in straight from coming off watch, fell into an immediate deep sleep, only to awake uneasy. Something was wrong. The porthole cover rendered the cabin pitch black, and the bunk rose and fell beneath me as the *Venetia* was tossed by turbulence. There was the familiar whoomphing of the seas crashing across the well-deck and yes … no hallucination, it was our siren. She was blowing continuous short blasts. Stevey appeared, and with his undentable exuberance yelled:

'Wakey wakey, Sparky,' and hauled me clean out of my bunk. I hit the floor and my ankle cracked against the bunkboard.

'You've broken my bloody ankle, you bloody idiot!' I cried in pain.

'That doesn't matter. You don't row with your legs.' Stevey pulled me upright. He took my greatcoat from the hook on the door and threw it over me.

'Get your things and come on deck. We're being attacked. It's the real thing. Move, Sparky, just move,' he urged.

He shot out. I donned jacket, coat, cap and scarf. I took my toothbrush and toothpaste and wrapped them in a handkerchief, and pocketed them along with a pair of scissors, just on a whim. I hurtled out into the alleyway and crashed into the chief steward, knocking him against the bulkhead. He wore a yellow oilskin hat that covered his ears and neck, and clutched a small briefcase. His mouth worked violently, fear making him a caricature. I was as scared as he but I had to smile. He half-raised his arm.

'I'll give you something to smile about,' he snarled. At that moment the mate appeared. He was furious.

'You two, get to your bloody boat stations at once!' I shot out and, bowing my head to the wind and spray, made my way to the radio cabin. Smith had reception on full volume. The phones were on the desk, the signals were so strong. He waved a hand for silence and logged another SSSS call.

'How many,' I asked.

'Three.' Smith turned to me tersely. 'Get to your boat station and don't carry your lifejacket, wear it. Go on.'

I went to the starboard boat-deck. Chippy and three seamen had swung the boat over the side, ready to be lowered into the sea. There were some fifteen men wearing their lifejackets, just waiting. They sat on wet planks, crouched, or leaned against bulkheads. They were silent, apart from the inevitable gallows humour. That was the worst thing of all, the waiting and the inability to do anything except hope.

'The army for me when I get home. Then, if Jerry pots at me I'll have a gun and can shoot back.'

'I'd like that bastard who spat in my beer to be here, now.'

'Why did he do that?'

'There were five of them, brown jobs. They kept taunting me for being a coward and not being in uniform, like they were. They came over and spat in my pint. Everyone else in the pub was hostile too, I could have been a criminal. I just left.'

'Why didn't you tell them you were in the Merchant Navy, man?'

'Why should I have to? Besides, we're civilians and the buggers have no idea what we're about.'

The ship trembled as the engines turned over at maximum revolutions. Pools of water gleamed on the well-deck. The scuppers belched and frothed with escaping water, and the wind bellied out the halyards, slapping colour into white faces and lashed waves over the *Venetia*'s plunging bows. Every time we rose on a crest we could see a small red patch astern, like a cigarette end glowing in a blacked-out street. It was a burning ship. We strained eyes to see what could be seen.

'Where's the destroyer?'

'She's got her hands full.'

'That burner is five miles astern ...'

'Closer. Three more likely.'

'Three. Five. What does it matter?' broke in a very petulant voice. 'Jerry knows we exist. The U-boats have more speed than we have. They can see us and we can't see them. There could be one lining up her periscope on us right now from any direction.'

The speaker was silenced by angry calls to shut up. No one spoke. There was wind, wetness and the groaning and straining of an old ship doing her best. More explosions were borne to us on the wind, depth charges according to Chippy. I was cold, tired and resigned. But, peculiarly, fear had gone. Mr Michaels had increased lookouts to watch for a torpedo wake or a U-boat surfacing.

'I'm dying for a smoke.'

'You dare, mate.'

'It was only a thought.'

'Better be.'

As men strained their eyes in all directions, imagination took over from sight. The former saw torpedoes in every streak of phosphorescence, in every speck of foam, whereas the latter saw varying shades of blackness.

'Hey, wake up, Ginger.'

Ginger, a Devonian able seaman from Barnstaple, protested.

'Stop shaking me! I've been on lookout, I've been at the wheel and I'm shagged out.'

The *Venetia* poised on the edge of a high swell, shuddered, slid down the trough and hit bottom with an impact that rocked her so violently that we had to cling to ventilators, rails, stanchions and one another. The less nimble fell. There were curses and laughter. I went to the radio cabin, as it had gone 2000 hours.

'I'll take my watch,' I said. Smith stayed seated and waved me away.

'I'll manage. You stand by the boat.'

'How many?'

'Still three, but they're still with us. Let's hope they've used up all their torpedoes. They won't be keen to surface with the destroyer about.'

As I reached the boat-deck there were four explosions quite close by. Then, another lot. Chippy said that once again they were depth charges. No one spoke; if the depth charges were close then it stood to reason that a U-boat could not be far away. A lookout called attention to the tongue of flame licking skywards about two miles to the south. We heard the muffled 'bong-bong' of a striking torpedo.

'Four,' I muttered.

'Four?' asked Johnny, standing next to me. I nodded. 'There could be others who couldn't get a distress call away?'

'Possible.'

The tongue of flame thinned into a bending stalk. A deep redness appeared at its base, a glow which swelled. Soon, there was only a scarlet bulbous patch, darkening by the minute.

The convoy ceased to exist the moment the first torpedo found its target. Sticking to plan, the surviving ships steamed flat out in all directions independently to escape the attack area, and head for their destinations alone. Mr Michaels had taken immediate control of the ship and stayed in the chartroom along with the mate and the helmsman. He pointed the *Venetia* away from the burning ship and when the depth charges erupted close by he again altered course. When another survivor, heading to cut across our path came dangerously close, he ordered a very abrupt turn to starboard. The *Venetia* yawed as she obeyed the wheel. We ran parallel with the other vessel, diverged and soon lost her. There were more depth charge explosions, fainter and to the north-east. The ship shuddered and vibrated as her engines were pushed to the limit and beyond.

We thought of several hundred seamen now dead, or pulling away in open lifeboats, or calling for help as they trod water or swimming, or just giving up and dying. There was nothing we could do to save them. Our job was to get our cargo of petrol and get it back to Britain. Of course, none of us looked at it that way at that moment. Our only instinct was to get away from the pack of Dönitz's 'grey wolves'.

There was an impatient knocking, like someone trying to raise a sleepy household. Well astern our lookouts reported gun flashes.

'Cheeky sod,' muttered someone. 'Surfacing with a destroyer about.'

'God help the Jerry who tangles with our gun crew.' We all laughed. Smith had been on radio watch for six hours and I went to take over. He looked remarkably cool and fresh. He told me to return to the boat-deck again. I protested but he was adamant.

Like the others I stared at the sea just in case I spotted that elusive torpedo wake.

'They also serve who stand and wait.'

'Pipe down with your bleeding Shakespeare, Wilkie.'

'Milton, you ignorant uneducated sod.'

'Bloody mystery man, you are,' vouchsafed a crouched deckhand.

More depth charges, very faint. The *Venetia* wallowed frantically as she responded to maximum revolutions and frequent turns of the helm. To me, then, with her safety linked to my own, she lived. We altered course to the west and the mood lightened. We felt we were clear of trouble. Then, a merchantman no more than a mile away was torpedoed. The explosion flash lit up the ocean and illuminated a wide area around, petrifying us. The flame died away leaving a blacker blackness than before. Mr Michaels gave the helmsman a sharp order and the mate moved quickly to help him wrench the wheel and the *Venetia* fell away as her well-deck veered towards the vertical. It was an impossible angle and I locked my arms around an adjacent ventilator and clung on hard. The ship dropped as she straightened and we hit bottom with a tremendous crash and torrents of water hit the well-deck. Solid spray hit our boat-deck, as if we were not already soaked enough. I heard someone yell out 'grab him'. The *Venetia* struggled back to an even keel and we heard more depth charges. Our engines belted and strained. I returned to the radio cabin.

'How many?'

'Five logged.'

'Let me take over.'

'Right. Another ten minutes.' I had to satisfy my curiosity.

'Have you ever had any trouble?' Smith threw me a quizzical look.

'I thought you'd never ask. The second month of the war. I was torpedoed. Then I joined the *Venetia*. Now, off you go. Come back in ten minutes.'

Back to the boat-deck. Regardless of the wet planking, the men were sprawling and sitting with heads bowed between knees, manifesting the exhaustion of emotions strained to the limit. All wore their neck-breakers. Some slept. Then, the mate joined us and said wearily;

'All right, lads. Keep your clothes on and your lifejackets handy and turn in.'

'Turn in?' came the peevish voice of Ginger. 'In a few minutes I'll be turned out again.'

Back in the radio cabin at 2200 hours ship's time. I offered to take the next six hours to equalise what Smith had done, but he refused, saying he would relieve me at midnight as usual, no arguments. I never dared argue with Smith; he was never unreasonable, never pulled rank or gave me the short straw, but was not backwards in telling me off when he thought I had let the department down. There was still a fence erected between us, but if that was what he wanted, fair enough.

Well, now I knew what the Battle of the Atlantic was really like. Our small convoy had lost six ships to torpedoes and a straggler. Doubtless, a top secret file in Whitehall would record the dry details; convoy number X in a certain position on a certain date was attacked and lost the following ships. Names, nationalities and gross tonnages would be noted. A bad loss of cargo space. Seamen? Tough, but of lesser importance.

I had trouble keeping awake. Smith relieved me spot on midnight, and we were back to normal watch. I collapsed on my bunk, only pausing to take off my neck-breaker. The lookout said he had a job waking me. The seas had moderated and we were alone. I thought of our erstwhile companion ships heading for destinations as far apart as Buenos Aires in the south and Montreal in the north. I missed the other ships; they had been something to look at. Now there would be the eternal seas and skies. No two things can be so beautiful in so many combinations, and yet so monotonous.

Westwards, with the ship's time being changed accordingly. Like all British ships at sea, no matter where, all our log entries adhered to Greenwich Mean Time. We were now dropping south-westerly down to the Caribbean and the weather improved day by day. The waves lost their bite and the friendly sun warmed and danced its sparkling rays on the waters. The underlying temperature rose steeply and the seamen working on deck stripped to the waist. Off-watch I would emulate them, turn my face to the sun and bask in its warmth.

Notwithstanding the upheaval of the past few days, the meals in the saloon were still edible. The main course was cold meats, and when my plate arrived Roy eyed my portion with the starved look of a hunter. For the first time a large jar of piccalilli mustard pickles appeared on the table, which surprised even the imperturbable mate, who patted the jar to see if it was real, threw it in the air, caught it, and replaced it with care as if it was a priceless Ming vase. Roy turned to the mate.

'Am I seeing things?'

'You certainly are, Roy.'

'Good-oh!' Our effervescent Aussie unscrewed the top of the jar and forked a small mound of the glistening golden contents onto his side plate. He was just about to eat a forkful when the captain arrived. He raised his eyebrows.

'There are others, Mr Garrett.'

Roy was unabashed. He said cheerfully,

'We can always get another jar, sir.' Nevertheless, under the Old Man's fierce scrutiny he forked the pickles back into the jar.

Others were not so lucky. We had a repeat performance of Wilkie and Mr Michael's disagreement over the food served to the inhabitants of the focsle, which had once again slumped in quality. Wilkie was once more threatened with logging, but stood his ground, and the chief steward paid another visit to the captain's quarters. The next day the galley wireless in the form of Stevey spread the news that the focsle had had its best rations since the voyage had started. Meanwhile, lunch in the saloon was a revelation, with two bowls of mixed salad and a dessert of tinned peaches and custard.

The radio never allowed us to forget the war. The occasional distress calls and the Rugby transmitter kept us alert. Because we were sailing independently from a convoy we were handed our position every thirty minutes. Stevey reported that the mate had called into the chief steward's office and had an intense low-key talk with him. The topic? The necessity of avoiding any more trouble over the food. We could not afford more trouble, not when we were alone and undefended.

One 1200 to 1600 hours watch, the *Venetia*'s vibrations slowed, then stopped. I heard hurried footsteps outside, peeped out and saw the chief engineer hurry back aft. I blew up the voice tube. Ian answered.

'Engine trouble, Sparky. We're stationary. The Old Man is hopping mad. Let's hope you don't have a chance to earn your pay.'

'How long will it take?'

'The chief says four hours at least. It's something to do with worn bearings and oil leakages. It has to be done.'

The engineers consulted their books on overtime pay and shot below. The chief donned his cap and white dungarees and joined them. It was very warm and the sea was calm. Some of those off watch became volunteer lookouts while they sunned themselves. Only the two marines on the gun platform aft longed to see a German target they could shoot at. No museum exhibit was ever so well greased and polished as their gun. Some of the hands berated their luck at having landed on such a clapped-out ship, but the bosun soothed them.

'This is a picnic, lads. Enjoy the sunbathing. If she breaks down when we're loaded, in the wrong place, then we could have something to worry about.'

It was nearly eight hours before we got underway again. I was on my 2000 to 2400 hours watch when I was relieved to feel that familiar vibrating underfoot. I looked out at the moon-kissed sea and quietly cheered. An hour later I was startled by a loud SSSS from a British merchantman. She had been struck by two torpedoes, had been split in two and was going fast. Her transmission was very loud. I voice-tubed up to the wheelhouse and gave her position to the mate. He whistled between his teeth.

'Praise the lord for our scrap yard engines, lad. She's barely six hours ahead on our set course.'

The mate alerted the captain, who was with him in a flash. They reasoned that it was sunk by one of the large transatlantic U-boats that lurked after easy pickings along the east coast sea route, and were fed by the German Type XIV milk-cow submarines which rendezvoused to re-fuel, re-arm and re-provision them. The mate was inclined to maintain course and, if no other ships had, pick up survivors. Mr Michaels was not so sure.

'If they got away in boats they'll survive. Scores of American coastguard stations and patrolling navy ships will have picked up their call. If we maintain course we're more likely to run into that damn submarine. And, Mr Parkinson, our prime task is to pick up our cargo and get it home. We'll turn eastwards and make a wide dogleg to bring us back on course by tomorrow morning.'

That is what we did. The helmsman reported the discussion to the focsle, and some were indignant that we had not steamed to pick up survivors. Others did back the captain's judgement as being the sensible course of action. Still, there was guilt felt as thoughts turned to the poor devils in the water. Chippy ruminated over the possibility that no-one would pick them up. Smith told the bosun to relay to the men that the American stations and warships kept reception on the 600-metre wavelength, and that if we had picked it up, so had many others.

Suddenly, the weather turned completely tropical. I sunbathed whenever possible during my daylight hours off watch, and was fascinated by the school of playful porpoises in the water. Flying fish soared across the surface of the sea and patches of gulf weed floated by. How they must have uplifted the spirits of ancient mariners, being a sign that land was nearby. They had the same effect on us, and we opened up doors and portholes wide. Mattresses, blankets and pillows were dragged outside to be heated by the sun, and across the well-deck men played cards, chess, draughts and dominoes, repaired their clothes or just yarned.

We picked up an SSSS from another British merchantman. It was sinking and being abandoned by its crew. Mr Michaels sent the *Venetia* on a prolonged zig-zag course. As we neared the Caribbean, electrical storms rendered reception almost impossible. There was increased interference from shore radio stations, but the dance music was very welcome. It became almost unbearably hot, but when I sat on watch in only my vest Smith told me standards had to be kept. I put my shirt back on as he lectured me about having respect for the job and myself.

Southwards, and twilights shortened. The cobalt ocean merged its horizon with the sky; we could have been alone in the centre of an enormous inverted blue bowl. Never before had I seen such starry skies, the large moon casting its fairy beam across the glistening water right to the ship. Johnny sighed that it looked like such a solid pathway that he was drawn to clamber over the side and walk on it.

'Don't try it,' I warned. 'If you ate today's duff you'll sink like a stone.'

'Soulless bugger,' said Johnny. He waved an encompassing hand and added, 'I'll bet you never saw nights like this in Hackney.' I had to agree with him.

The Virgin Islands slid by and the Atlantic was crossed. The crew were delighted by the squadrons of white gulls that welcomed us, heavy birds with a wide wing span and ungainly except in flight. Chippy sounded the number one fresh water tank and announced that it was down to sediment, and switched the supply to the number two tank. However, somehow it had become tainted, and its contents tasted like petrol. Boils, vomiting and general gastric upsets laid low many of the crew, and the captain had words with the mate for having allowed such carelessness to have gone unnoticed. The mate rebuked Ian, saying that he had told him to see to the tanks before leaving Shellhaven, and then Ian blamed Johnny for not having thoroughly cleaned both tanks before the *Venetia* sailed.

'Oh, I'll accept the buck,' retorted Johnny. 'When I get certificated I'll always be able to pass it onto some poor bloody apprentice.'

Stevey suffered excruciating pain from boils which appeared high up on the insides of his thighs. According to Stevey they were as large as ostrich eggs, but he declined to show us.

We glided past rocks rising sheer from the plate glass waters. Some had lighthouses on their highest points. We entered a convergence of sea lanes and saw many more ships, many of them neutrals with their large painted flags. With our blackouts up we looked like a poor relation. We came across a schooner, her white sails filled out by a gentle breeze as she hovered above the coppery waters.

The next day we altered course and raised a landfall ahead. It was an island and the *Venetia* was steaming straight for its centre.

'Aruba,' sighed the bosun happily. 'Dutch, and they're welcome to it. But there's beer ashore, Milwaukee and full of body and smooth to the gullet.' Johnny nudged me.

'And Hershey bars. We'll stock up for the trip back, Sparky.'

'You bet.'

Now, I had it all. A tropical island, blazing sun, glassy waters and cloudless skies. It was all I had read about, heard about and yearned for. Yet, my foremost thought was that I was halfway home.

7

ARUBA AND BERMUDA

Aruba. A sun-scorched island, one of a group of three Dutch dependencies, the others being Curaçao and Bonaire, lying strategically to the north of the Gulf of Venezuela. Its prosperity was linked to oil, which was why we were there.

At 0700 hours ship's time, 27 August 1940, I stood on the focsle head with Pablo Valdez and Dai Beaser and stared at the approaching port of St Nicholas. Few things in life can be as exhilarating as the anticipation of a young sailor preparing to go ashore in his first foreign port, especially if it is tropical. Our speed had come down to a dead slow as we moved through merchantmen swinging at anchor. Many were neutral, mostly American and Panamanian. Small maraicabo boats buzzed busily amongst them.

The previous day Smith had closed down the radio watch, enabling me to sit out in the sun in shorts and sandals, darning socks and sewing on buttons. I was also able to wage another war on the cockroaches that infested my cabin, attacking them with boiling soda water. My initial squeamishness at the sight of them had gone, but they still turned my stomach, even though I had grown used to eating fragments of them at every meal. It was astonishing how they sensed approaching danger and scurried off at great speed into the tiniest of crevices.

I saw little of Johnny. Amongst his many jobs was supervising two seamen in thoroughly cleaning out the troublesome water tanks and making them ready to take on fresh water as soon as we berthed. Stevey spent much of his time in the pantry with the chief steward, assessing what provisions would be required. He revealed that word from above had ensured that fresh and tinned fruit would be high on the list of requirements. Both the mate and the chief engineer had tackled the captain about dietary necessity and had managed to move the mountain.

A pilot launch came alongside and a Dutchman came aboard. He was beanstalk tall, blonde, heat-wilted and with a rancorous mien. He guided us to our berth alongside a long wide jetty, snatched a quick drink with Mr Michaels and hurried ashore. With the *Venetia* tied up a mere two-feet jump from the jetty, the craving to get ashore intensified. I longed to be able to walk and walk without being forced to zig-zag around railings, bulkheads and other obstacles. The crew became almost radiant, giving each other haircuts and arguing good-naturedly over a share of the washing lines and use of the clothing iron. The blow, because it was so unexpected, fell very heavily. The Dutch refused to issue shore passes for the rest of that day. Hands who were off duty and had been looking forward to a night ashore were indescribably bitter.

'Lousy squareheads. They can keep their dusthole and I'll keep my money.'

It was those who had already cleaned up and dressed in their best who felt most let down. As they watched the first enticing lights sprinkle the island their hopes of women, drink and some good food, in that order, were dashed. Their mutinous grumbles of going ashore and to hell with the consequences sent frissons of alarm through the deck officers. Some ten pairs of patrolling black policemen, all large and powerful, indicated that this had happened before.

No blackout. When the word passed around the ship every light, required or not, was switched on. For some men it was a way of letting off steam. The chief engineer bustled up to Mr Michaels and protested at the waste of electricity, but the captain politely declined to order any lights to be switched off. He was well tuned to the men's disappointment and had no wish to push any over the edge into reckless ship jumping. He asked the disgruntled engineer to have a drink with him, but the latter declined. In general, except where essential for the working of the ship, he conversed with no one – the mate, whom he regarded as his equal, being the exception.

Soon after breakfast the next morning I donned my long whites, signed for the ten dollars allowed to each member of the crew, collected my shore pass and went over the side. Johnny, Roy, Chippy and the bosun were busy with Aruban oil workers all over the well-decks. Hatch covers were being raised, hoses were being hauled aboard and two locals neatly dressed in white shirts and ties were walking about with clipboards. Before I went ashore I had gone to Smith's quarters, only to find him engrossed in a blueprint of his own making. He had told me to take the whole day off, saying he would go ashore in his own time.

The hot concrete burned through the thin leather soles of my white canvas shoes as I explored the island. The sun climbed and the heat rose, so that sweat soon soaked my vest and tunic jacket, but it was all a glorious release. I saw higgledy-piggledy houses, small shanty shops, fly-blown eateries and bars. I bought two oranges and peeled and ate them as I walked, then stopped a policeman and asked where the centre of St Nicholas was.

'Dis is it, sah.' He waved an encompassing arm around himself. I continued walking as if a giant mainspring was uncoiling itself inside, forcing me onwards. Dust trickled inside my jacket and

I wandered through clouds of flies and midges and through areas of shacks made from wooden packing cases and corrugated iron. Obese black women squatted in their doorways like good-humoured Buddhas. They were never idle, always working on garments or food preparations, as they ceaselessly chattered and called to one another.

American influence dominated the old Dutch colony. Its currency was the dollar and American goods, especially tinned foods and confectionary, filled its shops and stalls. The locals who spoke English did so with a southern drawl. For lunch I stopped at a small cafe and under a rattan roof had omelette and chips and drank an American beer. Heading back to the ship I was confronted by an enormous woman with shrewd piggy eyes and an incredibly wide smile. She thrust a stalk of bananas under my nose.

'One dollar, sah,' she lilted mellifluously. I shook my head. 'Fifty cents, den.' I shook my head again and tried to pass her, without success. She sighed dolorously. 'You're a hard man, sah. Very hard.' She thrust the bananas into my arms and sighed, 'all right. I agree, sah. I'll take a quarter.'

When I returned to the *Venetia* she was in the throes of loading. Huge notices in English and Spanish forbade smoking. As the fuel poured into her tanks the well-deck fell, levelled, then fell below the quayside. Johnny saw me come aboard and followed me into my cabin, where he proceeded to eat three bananas straight off. I ate two. They were succulent beyond belief and he asked for another, to which I nodded, and he ate two. He told me that loading was going without a hitch, and that we were being pushed out quickly. The stuff, he said, was badly needed at home. The mate had surprised everyone by blowing his top, which was very out of character. Seeing a young seaman stop work to light a cigarette, he had charged down the ship and smacked the lighter into the sea. He had then grabbed the offender by the shoulders, shaken him, then thrown him to the deck. After that the 'No Smoking' signs were superfluous. Everyone on deck worked in plimsolls or shoes with all-leather soles, and no hobnails or metal heel taps (or anything that could cause a spark) were permitted.

Later that afternoon an ebullient quintet comprising Stevey, Ray, Johnny, Ian and myself stepped ashore. Our mood was gay enough to be called light-hearted as Roy quipped;

'Chastity belts out and hide the keys, girls. Stevey is ashore, boils and all.'

The banter was non-stop. Since we broke out in sweat at the slightest movement we wandered into the first reasonably clean-looking bar in an effort to get out of the heat. I was owned by an elderly Armenian, from whom Stevey ordered five chilled Milwaukee beers.

'Make it four,' said Ian. 'I'll have an orange juice.'

Since we had missed the evening meal we called the Armenian over and asked whether he served food. I said that he did and that his wife and daughter were superb cooks. Stevey asked permission to go see the kitchen, and on his return declared that he would swap Maltese Johnny and the *Venetia*'s galley for what he'd seen. He ordered three fried eggs, a large well-cooked steak, onions and chips.

'You've missed out the fried tomatoes,' said Johnny.

'Oh yes, fried tomatoes,' added Stevey.

'What about mushrooms?' asked Ian. 'I like them.' Did the Armenians have mushrooms? They did, but in tins. We added mushrooms.

'How about a couple of bangers?' said Roy. Did they have sausages? They did. Were they pork sausages, I asked. They were.

'In that case add two sausages to the others and give me an extra half portion of steak,' I said.

'Baked beans?' ventured Roy.

'Not bloody likely!' the rest of us said in unison.

We sat at a table next to a withered ten-foot plant dying in its terracotta pot, and enjoyed our feast. It was surprisingly good. We drank more chilled beer and orange juice and, feeling compassionate, shared some with the pot plant. During the course of the meal the bar filled up with a smattering of local residents and seafarers. There were Canadians, Scandinavians, Frenchmen and a mixture of Allied Europeans and South and North Americans. We all sat at the crude wooden tables with the unhurried air of men who had time to kill until they steamed away. The bosun and Chippy came in and joined us, and more drinks followed. We watched some randy Americans pester the Armenian as to the location of women, and when he shrugged negatively for the umpteenth time and they still felt he was holding out on them, he moved back behind the bar. Another party of Americans who were rather aggressively drunk looked like coming to blows with some Brazilians, at which point the proprietor surreptitiously but speedily put up framed wire netting to protect his bottles and glasses. Roy suddenly stood up.

'Well, there's damn all going on in this place,' he exclaimed. 'I'm going for a walk. Coming?'

We all joined him, apart from Ian, who rushed back to the ship for his spell of duty. Johnny and I then sloped off on a food buying expedition, managing to stock up on chocolate bars, chewing gum, tinned fruit and fresh fruit, mainly oranges, grapefruit and nuts. We each filled a sizeable bag. On our way back to the *Venetia* we passed by the bosun and Chippy, hard at work seriously drinking. Back aboard Johnny reported to the mate and I played chess with Pablo under the bright arc lights that lit up the whole length of the ship. It was rumoured that we would set sail on the high tide next evening at 1900 hours.

I went ashore in the morning with Johnny. We pooled the last of our cents and bought boiled sweets and shelled brazil nuts. In the afternoon the bosun and Chippy went ashore for a last bout of drinking. Streetwise Stevey crossed his fingers and said:

'I do hope the bosun doesn't go over the top. When he's in a mood for a bender only unconsciousness can stop him bending the elbow.'

The ship did not sail as planned. The Dutch pilot came aboard and sat in Mr Michaels' quarters, smoked his pipe and drank, but did not guide us out of harbour, because four men were missing. He assured the captain that he didn't mind our extended stay, since Gow, Harrison and Company would foot the bill for his overtime.

The mate hastened ashore with Ian to find the missing men. One, surprisingly, was the bosun. The mate engaged the help of the police in the search, and meanwhile the engineers kept up steam, ready for a quick getaway. Mr Michaels walked round and round the lower bridge, tight-lipped and furious. Roy found a very upset Chippy and asked why the bosun had not returned with him.

'He just wouldn't,' said Chippy. 'In fact, we left that place together and then he peeled away and said he would be along soon afterwards. I should have stayed with the silly bugger.'

Sailing that evening was abandoned. The pilot went ashore and arranged to return before dawn to catch the tide. It was around 2300 hours when the mate and Ian, aided by four policemen, turned up with the miscreants. They were Mandel the Pole, Derek Kenny the red-haired Welshman, Charlie Smith who was a greaser from Wolverhampton, and the bosun. The police pushed them down the gangway, which now sloped down to the well-deck due to the increased weight our cargo gave us, shook hands with the mate and Ian and went onto the quayside to watch developments. Mr Michaels had gone into his quarters and changed, and he appeared in full white uniform complete with brass hat, epaulettes, each with four gold bars, and two rows of medals from the First World War. He stood ramrod straight, motionless, and then he started to berate the very drunk sailors.

'Drunken, besotted, irresponsible, good-for-nothing disgraces to the merchant service! Dipsomaniacal crapulous gutter sweepings! You have delayed a ship in wartime carrying a vital cargo ...' His enunciation was theatrically clear. His voice started quietly and rose and rose, attracting the attention of seamen on other ships, the policemen on the quayside and passersby. The garish arc lights lit up the scene with a yellow brilliance and the errant four huddled together on the well-deck as Mr Michaels continued to pour verbal fire and brimstone onto their befuddled heads, until he concluded with the words;

'You are logged one pound apiece.'

That broke their spell. Considering their wages, it was not an inconsiderable sum. Charlie Smith broke away from the others and scrambled up the bridge companionway towards the captain. His eyes were staring and spittle drooled down his chin. The rotgut he had imbibed on shore combined with a deep sense of grievance looked set to snap all restraint. Mr Michaels waited until Charlie's head came level with the lower bridge deck and then he calmly stepped forward, placed his foot against the greaser's shoulder and pushed hard. Charlie arched backwards and fell on the well-deck with an almighty thud. As he lay there, spread-eagled on his back, the whole ship and the many spectators on the jetty heard Mr Michaels utter one word:

'Trash.'

Charlie moaned and raised himself on all fours. He shook himself like a dog coming out of the sea, ran his hand gingerly over the back of his head and stared at blood. We all thought he had sobered up, and perhaps he had, but nevertheless he picked up a steel wedge and hurled it at Mr Michaels. It missed his head by about a foot, made a tremendous clang and bounced off into the water. The captain had not moved an inch, even though the wedge would have killed him had it struck home. Charlie Smith stood still, swaying slightly, the brainstorm over, all fight gone.

98

'Take that rubbish forward. And another pound logging for assault on a ship's officer.'

'Bastard!' yelled Charlie. As he bent to pick up another missile Wilkie ran forward and grabbed him round the waist, pinioning his arms. The greaser struggled with a frenzy that the powerful Wilkie could barely contain. Pablo rushed to help him, so did Harry Reed and Ginger. They hauled the struggling man back to the focsle.

During the ruckus the bosun had stalked off the ship onto the jetty and was pacing back and fro declaring that the *Venetia* would have to find another bosun, and that he was not going back. Mr Michaels stared wearily at him and called down to him to come aboard. But the bosun continued his pacing, his face glowing with alcohol, sweat and indignation. His actions put the captain in a quandary, as it was obvious that he had no wish to impose further fines, but after another call, to which the bosun responded with one of his own for the captain to go to hell, Mr Michaels had no choice. He logged the bosun another pound. The mate nodded to the captain, who returned to his quarters, and he and Chippy went onto the jetty to cajole the bosun back on ship. They took him to the mate's cabin and poured coffee into him, and talked like old seadogs. Through the early hours of the night groups of men talked and, as is the compassionate way of a ship's company towards one of their own, they raised the money to pay the extra fines of both the bosun and Charlie Smith.

The *Venetia* sailed at dawn, and I was awakened by the sun streaming through my cabin's open porthole. I slipped on shorts and shirt and went on deck to see the disappearing town of St Nicholas. Homeward bound, two words that have delighted seafarers for centuries. I could sense the happy atmosphere that permeated the ship. Even the chief steward greeted me with a 'nice morning, Sparky,' to which I replied in kind. Stevey informed me that the normal radio watch would resume at noon, and that as Mr Michaels would attend breakfast I would have to wear my long whites.

I realised I had not seen Smith at all while we were berthed. He had gone ashore alone, and no one knew where he went or what he did. He had certainly not been seen in the usual stomping grounds of the regular seamen.

Breakfast was a strange affair. Mr Michaels was in a strange mood, almost as if the previous night's drama had never happened. He had gained respect for his courage from many for having watched that metal wedge coming at him and never flinching. He even became loquacious, telling the story of a perilous affair he had had with a milliner's daughter in Hamburg, when he had been a third mate. It was not the episode itself which made us smile appreciatively as much as the thought of the captain cooing in faulty German in his thick Scottish accent.

The *Venetia* curved northwards through the transparent glassy Caribbean. Low down in the water due to the weight of our cargo, we showed a bare two feet of freeboard and the occasional heads of water threw tinsel spray over the well-deck.

'She'll be a bugger in the north Atlantic,' warned Johnny. 'Most of the time you'll have to use the flybridge to move about.'

Metal became too hot to touch and all through the heat the seamen hosed down the well-deck. No one smoked out on deck and the deck officers and bosun spot-checked footwear. We carried 80% octane petrol. There was debate as to how many Spitfires it could keep flying and for how many hours. As no one knew the fuel consumption of the aircraft it was an argument in the dark, but it helped pass the time.

At noon Smith went on watch and the golden sun soared high and turned the sea to liquid fire that hurt the eyes. The crew settled easily into their working routine, even the four Aruba absentees. The engineers erected a large canvas awning aft to protect us from the sun, and at night many slept on deck. It grew still hotter and the mate said that he had never known it so warm in these parts. The radio cabin was a sweat box; when I rested my elbows on the desk they left pools of perspiration. But I had to be on alert. We were back on a war footing, even though we criss-crossed with various neutrals, mostly Americans and Panamanians.

I was thinner, the holes of slack in my belt increasing from four to six, but I felt tremendously fit. Johnny and I had little feasts and the nuts, tinned fruit and bananas diminished rapidly. As the Hershey bars had almost liquidised we put them in a cool place until we hit cold weather.

The engine room staff suffered most of all and none could endure four hours below without coming on deck for a breath of fresh air in the shadiest spot and a drink of water. Some stripped naked and were squirted with the water hoses. Jones, the elderly greaser, collapsed and was carried up and placed under the aft awning. Mr Michaels gave the chief engineer salt tablets to distribute amongst the men and unlimited access to fresh water. Jones, despite his protests, was made to take two days off work. His mates shouldered the extra toil without complaint.

They galley wireless, always eerily accurate, spread the word that we were heading for Bermuda to join a homeward-bound convoy. Steering a northerly course we found ourselves in a cooler and choppier Atlantic. Static interference made radio reception very difficult, but we picked up two SSSS calls not too far east, in the Cape Verde basin. There, German milk-cow submarines re-supplied U-boats, and the mate said that our course would cut across the U-boat rendezvous and their American coast ambush areas. We started to zig-zag as the radio transmissions from GBR Rugby started to come in loud and clear. They warned of an armed raider on the loose, and gave areas to be avoided and diversions to be made. GBR made us aware that we were approaching the killing zones.

On board, our cargo was a taboo subject, but we talked generally about the cargoes merchant seamen preferred to avoid. There were ammunition and explosive carriers, which would blow up if torpedoed, fuel tankers which would flame, grain ships whose swelling cargoes could burst them apart, and, most feared of all, scrap metal and ore carriers, which would go down in minutes. Long John, the ex-ballroom dancer, had been working on deck when a torpedo struck his ore carrier, and it had gone down like a lift, leaving him one of a handful of survivors picked up by a rescue sloop trailing the convoy. It was amazing how many of the *Venetia*'s crew had already been torpedoed, mined, bombed and sunk. A few more than once.

The chief steward had not over-provisioned in Aruba. The initial glorious fresh fruit and salad had reduced in two days to just fruit. Then the choice of the latter dwindled to one orange per man. To make matters worse the food generally became inedible, then Maltese Johnny went down with a fever. Mr Michaels visited the stricken cook, and as a result Stevey was to be seen taking him a tumbler filled with a greenish concoction and some large reddish pills.

'He's a lousy cook, but not even he deserves that,' said Roy.

The galley boy, a pimply bespectacled youth from Bermondsey generally known as 'Einstein' because of his intelligent look, became the cook. His culinary skills extended to peeling potatoes, badly, and an ability to fork suicidal cockroaches out of the cooking pots. The ship-wide roar of protest after his first meal forced the Old Man to take action, and since Stevey had often boasted about his cordon bleu cooking skills, he now paid the price for his boasting. He was rather dismayed at being named cook, but aided by the relieved galley boy he did his best. We felt a certain glee at watching the furious chief steward acting as waiter in Stevey's place, but the food was still terrible. Mr Michaels paid Maltese Johnny another visit, and the next day a shaky cook was back in the galley, albeit drinking the green concoction three times a day, but his fever soon disappeared after much sweating in the heat of the kitchen.

Once we had cleared the shipping lanes Mr Michaels gave the gunners permission to have a shoot, even going so far as to joke that they had better have practice in case we met a German pocket battleship. Chippy lashed four large planks across empty oil drums and gave the makeshift raft a mast flying a large white bunk sheet. Bets were struck everywhere, usually an even five shillings, as to whether or not the gunners would score. There would be four shots of live shells. The marine sergeant happily gave last minute instructions to his motley crew; they included the other young marine, Harry Reed, two seamen and Billy Boy, the engineers' chirpy Liverpool-Irish steward. Just below the gun platform Chippy and Ginger held the target poised on the rail. The sergeant raised his arm, a hearty push and the target fell into the water. It almost vanished in the creamy wake, re-surfaced and fell rapidly astern. Every binocular and eye was trained on it. The gun crew fired four shots, and loud cheers greeted each shell burst with observations like 'there goes the poor old *Bismarck*'.

The shoot over, the mate ruminated on the blown-in side of the deck house and two cracked engine skylights. Two of the shots had fallen close enough to start arguments, some saying that they had seen pieces of timber and oil drum flying into the air, while those who had bet against the marines accusing the optimists of needing to get their eyes checked. Roy's suggestion that we turn the ship around to go check was not taken up.

The next morning Johnny and I had just shared our last tin of peaches when Wilkie looked through the porthole.

'Aha. What are you two scallywags up to?'

'Chin-wagging,' said Johnny. 'Come in.'

'Heavens, inviting a focsle rat into an officer's cabin?'

Johnny looked at me. 'Shall I let the rat into my cabin?'

'For a price. Two mugs of tea.'

'Blackmailers.' Wilkie disappeared, and within five minutes returned with tea.

'How did you manage that?' I asked.

'I have an understanding with the cook,' smiled Wilkie. 'If I want something within reason and the chief steward is out of sight, I get it.' He spotted the omnibus of Shakespeare's plays, which I had taken from the saloon library some three weeks earlier, and pounced on it. 'Aha, an oasis of literature amidst a desert of Zane Grey westerns and True Murders.' Then he surprised us by reciting soliloquies and sonnets off by heart. He could even quote the pertinent character, play and act.

'Where did you learn all that?' I asked.

'In Dublin.' Wilkie lit a cigarette and held it in cupped hands. 'I was a leading light in the university theatricals. Then I joined a company which toured all over Ireland. We even played on the mainland, that's why I can stand up to that old bastard on the lower bridge. I can transpose myself to being on stage and playing a part, I can face him out.'

'What on earth are you doing in the *Venetia*'s focsle …'

'That's another story,' Wilkie hesitated, then said 'domestic. My wife was having an affair while I was away on tour. I came home a day early in the afternoon, and found them on the job. I always did have a short fuse. I beat the poor sod so badly that they thought he would snuff it. He didn't. Not quite. The police charged me with attempted murder but they were careless. I got away and friends helped me to get across to England. I signed on a ship at Birkenhead three years ago and here I am. The world outside dear old Erin is a large enough place. I'll never go back. Correction … I can't go back. My name, then, was not Wilkie.'

Before he left he told us not to talk about his past to anyone. We promised, and never did reveal Wilkie's story.

Radioed instructions had us zig-zagging through a long stretch, which raised the hoary old argument as to whether an alteration to port was a zig or a zag. A most enormous spread of weed wrapped itself around the *Venetia*'s bows, but the bridge refused to slow or stop to loosen it. Instead, the bosun and a seaman spent nearly an hour dislodging it with two long poles. We picked up the occasional flying fish that landed on the well-deck; grilled they reduced to a couple of mouthfuls and tasted like herrings.

Smith picked up a distress call from a Dutch merchantman and I had an SSSS the following watch. The food remained poor and Stevey reported that two seamen were keeping daily records of what they received and intended to give the report to the National Union of Seamen.

'Fat lot of good they can do in peacetime,' commented Chippy, 'let alone in wartime.'

On the evening of Wednesday 14 September we sighted Bermuda. We dropped to half speed and a launch came out to meet us and signalled by aldis that we would have to cruise outside around Murray's anchorage. We cursed, as it meant that we would have to maintain all watchkeeping and lookouts. I kept the 0400 to 0800 hours watch, had breakfast and a sleep, and when I awoke the ship's engines were stilled. We were at anchor off Hamilton.

'Last lap to home,' I said to Johnny. He gave me an old-fashioned look.

'Aye, that it is. But, Sparky, it's a hell of a lap.'

There was no shore leave, which was especially painful given that Bermuda looked such a pleasing contrast to Aruba, being green, cultivated, like a piece of Sussex countryside broken away from the mainland. The white mansions set amidst the verdant hills sloping down to the sea smacked of affluence and tranquility. Again, we felt like the kids in the Bisto advertisement, their noses pressed longingly against a bakery window filled with delectable but unobtainable pastries.

Bermuda was the main southern Atlantic terminus for ships. It scooped in merchantmen from every North and South American port and from far beyond, and pushed them out in Britain-bound convoys. Every day there were arrivals; refrigerated meat carriers from the Argentine and Uruguay, tankers, freighters carrying wood and food from the Antipodes, timber ships from British Columbia, and vessels laden with general cargoes of chemicals, guns, vehicles, munitions, scrap metal and every commodity that a beleaguered island nation needed for survival. Our third day there we watched a twenty-four-ship convoy move it. It was escorted by a lone merchant cruiser.

In 1939 the Admiralty took over some seventy passenger liners and converted them into merchant cruisers. They were used to fill the gaps left by a hard-pressed and thinly stretched Royal Navy, even though their thin skins made them ill-equipped for the military tasks allotted to them. Each was commanded by a Royal Navy officer and crewed by merchant seamen. A major function of these AMCs was escorting trans-Atlantic convoys. The erstwhile civilian seamen soon adapted to naval demands, like forming gun crews, and whenever necessary they acquitted themselves well and with gallantry.

The two most famous AMCs were the *Rawalpindi* and the *Jervis Bay*. On 23 November 1939 the *Rawalpindi* was patrolling a line between Iceland and the Faroes when it was found by the German battleship the *Scharnhorst*. Three times the *Scharnhorst* ordered the *Rawalpindi* to heave to, and three times she refused. The German was then joined by her sister ship, the *Gneisenau*, and together they blew the *Rawalpindi* out of the water. There were very few survivors. One year later, on 5 November 1940, the *Jervis Bay* was solely protecting a convoy of thirty-seven merchantmen who were homeward bound from Halifax. Late that afternoon they were sighted by the German battleship *Admiral Scheer*. To save his ships as they scattered and steamed flat in all directions, the Royal Navy captain of the *Jervis Bay*, Captain Edward Fegen Fogarty, committed his crew, his ship and himself on a suicide course. He turned to challenge the German raider, steaming at her and firing guns. He had no chance. Massive broadsides from the *Admiral Scheer* set the *Jervis Bay* aflame from end to end and sank her. Later, a handful of survivors were picked up by a Swedish ship, but Fogarty had been killed. He was awarded a posthumous Victoria Cross. His gallant action, which attracted all the fire and attention of the Germans, bought sufficient time for the merchantmen to lose themselves in darkness. The battleship did manage to pick off five Red Dusters but thirty-two escaped. The actions of the *Jervis Bay* had prevented a slaughter of the defenceless.

The weather off Bermuda was perfect, warm, tempered by a constant crossing breeze. Boredom reigned once more and the bosun had the seamen over the sides on cradles to complete red leading and painting. Johnny helped me to launch another assault on the cockroaches in my cabin, and I reciprocated. Washing lines went up again outside the focsle. Chippy placidly made his wooden animals for his wife to sell and Long John surprised everyone by producing a flute and playing it with professional aplomb. Smith read and spent much time puzzling over his personal radio circuit. Mr Michaels, according to Stevey, read and wrote in his foolscap books while he waited for the launch to take him ashore to the convoy conference along with the other master mariners whose ships would be our companions. Dai Beaser continued his efforts to convert me to communism; he failed, but was always logical.

'It all depends on your birth, Sparky. If you're born into a wealthy aristocratic family and lack for nothing except how to pass the time – should I got hunting today, or to the casino, or to the club for lunch or to tea and cakes at Harrods – then you are a Tory. You defend what God has given you. And revolutionaries like the communists who want to deprive you of your luck are the enemy. But, if you are born into a large poor family in an area where the dole queues are endless and you can't see the light at the end of the tunnel you have nothing to lose by revolution. So I joined the Communist Party and, come the revolution, me and mine will be better off.'

The proximity of shore was tantalising. Through the much-in-demand binoculars we could see the details of houses, people walking about, the fields and the trees and the colourful blooms and even the occasional tennis match. In the clear water fish were abundant. There were the groper and garfish and the occasional languid snapper, which would flit to the surface. The bosun wagered Wilkie that he could catch a snapper, and the latter accepted the bet. The bosun hastened aft and returned with a Heath Robinson harpoon. It was a metal stanchion honed to a point and bolted to a two-inch by two-inch length of wood to give it stability. A stout line was fastened through a drilled hole at the top of the wood and ended in a loop that went over the bosun's wrist. An interested group gathered around to watch.

First, the bosun emptied a large tin of crumbs and meat scraps from the galley into the water. The feast immediately drew a shoal of tiny fish to the surface, and the bosun took careful aim and hurled his harpoon down at them. He stunned quite a number and scooped up a quantity with a long-handled net. From them he sorted out half a dozen, threw the rest back into the sea and carefully wired the still-wriggling fish together. He carefully lowered the moving ball of bait into the sea and almost immediately a large snapper rose lazily towards it. He straightened, took aim, and threw the harpoon with all his strength down at the prize. It was a good shot, and the harpoon either killed the snapper outright or stunned it with shock. However, it drifted away just out of range of his net and was set upon by other fish and quickly devoured. Wilkie collected his pound bet and I had my fill of fishing.

Smith told me to give the batteries, aerials and insulators a final thorough overhaul before we set off back across the Atlantic. Straight after breakfast I got stuck into the job, checking the specific gravities of all the wet cells in the batteries, topping up with distilled water where required, scraping the metal terminals and their bulldog grip connections clean until they gleamed and protecting them all with loathsome black grease. My hands and forearms became covered in dirt, but back down in my cabin I found that my weekly ration of soap was down to a useless sliver. I knocked at the chief steward's door in trepidation; there was an illogical antagonism between us.

'What he bloody hell do you want?' was his immediate question. 'Look! You've got grease on my door!'

'I'm sorry, I'll wipe it off. I need more soap.'

'You've had your ration for the week,' he smirked. 'Two days before you get another bar.' I displayed my arms and hands and explained what I had been doing. He replied, 'That's your bad luck. You can't have another tablet.' I persisted, and the argument became more acrimonious until the mate emerged in his dressing gown.

'What the hell is this about?' he said angrily. I told him the situation and showed him my arms and hands. He told me to return to my cabin, which I did, and fell asleep on my bunk in a foul temper. When Stevey awoke me for lunch there was a new bar of soap in my sink.

That evening an armed merchant cruiser slipped into the anchorage and next morning Mr Michaels, wearing his full whites and clutching a briefcase, was collected by a launch and taken ashore. After breakfast a large chandler's launch came alongside the lowered gangway and a merry half-caste salesman with two boy assistants boarded the *Venetia* and laid out their wares along the well-deck. There were Bermudan souvenirs, tropical clothing and seafaring clobber. These were mostly ignoring, but we all bought bunches of bananas and other fruit, boiled sweets and chocolate bars. Everyone bought sugar. It was rationed at home but out here a pound weight cost two and a half pence. I paid for two sackfuls, each weighing twenty pounds. Stevey, as instructed by Mr Michaels, bought eight sackfuls. The bosun toyed wistfully with a thick cotton country and western shirt, put it back and said,

'I blew all my dough in Aruba.'

'Aye, you did that you bloody idiot, and I saw you do it,' agreed Chippy. He winked at the onlookers. They had a whip round and the bosun got his shirt. He was genuinely embarrassed by the gift.

8

RUNNING THE GAUNTLET

On Sunday 8 September 1940, at 0800 hours ship's time, we upped anchor and slowly moved out to sea. We formed part of a single file of ships. Ahead was a Dutch freighter of some 7,000 gross tonnage, very low down with large crates lashed to her decks. Behind was a British tanker, a San boat. Johnny stared at it reflectively. It was on a San boat that his father had perished. Another San boat, the *San Demetrio*, achieved fame. On her way home she was torpedoed and set aflame, and survivors promptly ran for the lifeboats. After several hours of rowing they sighted a ship, but when they got close they were amazed to see that it was the *San Demetrio* herself, still miraculously afloat. They clambered back on board and found it fire-gutted and in a dangerous fume-filled state, so that lighting a match to start the galley stove was an act of heroism in itself. After a perilous voyage they succeeded in bringing home both the ship and her valuable cargo. A book was later written about the story of the brave crew and the unsinkable vessel, which was later made into a film.

Wisps of smoke rose from sun-blistered funnels. Pennants flew on halyards. Launches cut in and out delivering messages and on the twenty-four ships some 2,500 merchant seamen became afflicted by homeward-bound exuberance. The receding island of Bermuda still looked green and inviting but it had been a barren place for all the enjoyment the ship's company had derived from it. We were flying pennants two and five, which denoted that we were to be the second ship in the fifth column, an outside one, which we did not relish. There was much argument as to which position in the convoy would be the safest, but the real answer was that no position was safe, or safer, or safest. The German Admiral Karl Dönitz had put paid to that with his system of U-boat coordination, the *rudeltaktiken*, pack tactics, which brought together up to a dozen submarines. Every man in our convoy was aware that our main defence was luck. Only luck, or lack of it, would count.

Outside in the open glassy waters twenty-four belly-filled iron containers manoeuvred laboriously and in due course every ship was settled in its correct station. The armed merchant cruiser sauntered out to join us. As she approached to take up position in the centre of the convoy she seemed to give her charges a critical once over. With our engines just ticking over and the crew raring to go we were like a bunch of athletes in the starting blocks waiting for the gun. Our bridge lookout yelled;

'Hoist!'

All ships repeated the commodore's flag signal. Sirens tooted. Funnels coughed out bursts of grimy smoke, evoking a warning signal from the commodore that dirty giveaway smoke would not be tolerated. Wakes feathered behind churning screws and we were under way. We ran up our red B flag as did seven other ships carrying volatile and explosive cargoes. These included a Norwegian tanker on our port beam and a British tanker two stations astern of us.

'Sometimes Sparky, I don't like the company we keep,' commented Roy.

Bermuda disappeared into a flat haze as the enormous red sun fell below the horizon, and with encroaching darkness the gem island was completely lost to view. News brought back by Mr Michaels from the convoy conference suddenly sobered us all. The Luftwaffe had been bombing England ferociously, especially London. I thought of bombs falling on my family home in Amhurst Road, Hackney, and it was Johnny's turn to cheer me up with a precious banana and a cup of tea.

At noon I re-opened the radio watch. As we set a north-easterly course Ian called down the voice tube and gave me the first position. The next day onwards the bridge would give us our position every half an hour. The familiar and comforting Rugby transmitter was still sending out its coded messages ordering ships to avoid areas where aircraft and U-boats were active. The first cockroach scurried across the bulkhead and I flicked an elastic band at it, but missed. Smith came in for an uncharacteristic chat. He had heard about my spat with the chief steward over the bar of soap, and I expected a rebuke. To my surprise he took my side and said that if I had come to him he would have tackled Mr Twitch himself. Before leaving he said:

'Do some more practice transmitting on the dead key. One can go through the war without having to transmit but, if it happens, your speed and accuracy could save lives, including your own.'

Our convoy continued making north and east. The weather cooled and the skies became greyer with a patchwork of mottled cloud cover. A flecked choppiness replaced the tropical smoothness of the seas and water continually sloshed onto the well-deck. Hosing down ceased, but the smoking ban remained, and the bosun still spot-checked footwear. The weight of the *Venetia*'s cargo made her movements slower and more predictable, giving her a rocking lullaby motion.

Longitude 55 degrees west and more cloud. Fewer stars were visible at night and a stiff wind sprang up and did not relent. High-crested rollers began chasing through the convoy lanes and speed dropped to six knots. Homeward bound every ship was worth its weight in peacetime gold for the war effort because of its cargo, and our escort did not want to risk a single one unless left without option. Three times in three days an ancient Greek, the SS *Adamis*, fell out with engine trouble. As we were ordered to slow our speed to allow her to catch up she became the most hated ship in the convoy. When it happened again on the fourth day the commodore ordered her back to Halifax in Nova Scotia. We never saw her again. Such is the strange fellowship of seafarers towards one another that our cursing of the Greek turned into hoping that she made port safely.

The next day the *Empire Unity* broke down. She signalled by aldis to the commodore that she had a boiler leak. We watched her fall astern and put paid to seeing her again, but she made repairs and caught us up some eight hours later and took up her station.

Twice a week when I came off watch at midnight I walked along the flybridge to play chess with Pablo. He said I was doing well. He gave me a well-thumbed English-Spanish language book. I studied this in my cabin and on watch and it accelerated my ability to converse in Spanish no end. Sometimes, when I left Pablo, I stood on the flybridge and gazed at the moonlit ships silhouetted against the stars. A wonderful sight, and wonderful targets. Blackout on all ships was impeccable, I never saw a chink of light or the flash of a lighter, but there was little you could do about the moon.

At longitude 45 degrees west the interference from American radio stations faded completely and bang went my jazz and dance music. Inevitably, discontent over food flared up again. What we were given in the saloon had got pretty bad, but the grumbles from the focsle were incessant. Then, Maltese Johnny made a stew for lunch known as 'lobscouse'. It had been a staple stomach-filler on sailing ships and steamers running to and from the ports of Liverpool and Hamburg, made of meat, potatoes, onions and assorted vegetables. With fresh ingredients and well cooked it must have made a tasty dish, but Maltese Johnny produced one of his real culinary disasters. For the fourth time during the voyage Wilkie led a deputation along the flybridge to complain, made up of Charlie Smith and Ginger. They walked past the amidships and made their way to the galley. Seeing them come Maltese

Johnny retreated inside, slamming the bottom half of the steel door and bolting it from the inside. Charlie Smith leaned over it and thrust a large tray of brown sludge under the frightened cook's nose.

'Do you know what is the tastiest thing in this muck?' Johnny just stared at him, his hand grasping a steel frying pan. 'The cockroaches!' exploded Charlie, 'the bloody cockroaches!'

'What can I do?' protested the cook, as Wilkie laid a restraining hand on Charlie's arm. 'I make what I'm told. "Give them a stew" he says, and what do I get? Meat so maggoty it walks, potatoes so long in storage they're sprouting and carrots and onions so mouldy they're fit only for pigswill.'

'Come,' said Wilkie, and he led his supporters back amidships. Alone, he took a tray of lobscouse and knocked on Mr Michaels' door. The captain emerged in an irascible mood.

'Well?'

'You promised to see that the food would improve,' said Wilkie.

'That I did, Mr Wilkie.'

'Did you? Sir?' Mr Michaels swelled with exasperation.

'Damn you, sir. I have a mind to make things very difficult for you.' The Old Man was aware of the anger caused by the poor food, but he was of the old school where ships' captains could rule their roosts with iron fists. He could not change, and he told Wilkie to step down and take his deputation with him.

Wilkie's control snapped. The comfortless life, lack of privacy, the hard endless routine, our dangerous cargo and the enemy gauntlet we had to run wore nerves thin. Good warm food to look forward to was a precious thing. He threw a tray overboard, which showered the lower bridge and the well-deck with large blobs of brown mess.

'You are logged two pounds for damage to company property,' announced Mr Michaels.

'This isn't sixty years ago!' shouted Wilkie. 'You can't treat seamen like hired oxen, we have a right to decent living conditions, which you can't do anything about on this stinking rustbucket, but you can do something about the food.'

For a long time the two men stared eyeball to eyeball and then Mr Michaels compressed his lips into a thin bloodless line.

'I will speak to the chief steward. Now go forward with your men.'

The ritual took place again. Stevey went to the chief steward, who appeared ten minutes later at the captain's quarters. He was out in two minutes, a furiously unhappy man. The next day salad and tinned fruit appeared on the saloon table. The meat was less tough and the vegetables were fresher. Dai commented that we should all chip in and pay Wilkie to beard Mr Michaels once a week.

Latitude had climbed from 10 degrees north to over 50. Now level with southern England we still headed north towards Iceland. Old hands speculated that we were going to sneak around the northern extremities of the U-boat patrol lines strung along the latitude 30 degrees west. No one knew. Those ashore who directed ship and convoy movements necessarily played their cards close to their chests. In this game, careless talk did cost lives and, more importantly, valuable cargoes.

The weather turned very cold, almost arctic. High winds chilled the ill-dressed very quickly and drove menacing combers through the convoy, pummelling ships as they struggled to maintain speed and station. The *Venetia* rolled and climbed and dropped into troughs with heart-stopping thuds. The well-decks were seldom free of knee-deep waters and the mate issued orders that all hands had to use the flybridge unless they had work elsewhere. Spray, as high as monkey-island, raked across from stem to stern and mufflers, sweaters, sou'westers and even thigh boots became the order of the day.

At longitude 40 degrees west and latitude 56 degrees north a Geordie tramp, a Souter Line boat, loaded to the limit of her elastic plimsoll line, put up black balls and fell behind. The commodore ordered her to make for Nova Scotia if she could not regain us. Smith and I added to the file of torpedoed ships. There was an unusual, straightforward SOS distress call, some 200 miles to the east, of a Britisher foundering with a serious engine breakdown.

'How can ships like that be allowed to leave a home port without proper inspection and a seaworthy certificate?' I asked Harry Reed.

'Because it's wartime, Sparky,' he said. 'Many ships now at sea were saved from being scrapped. The country needs every ounce of cargo we can bring come. So, when we return and unload, we're being pushed out to sea again as quickly as possible without the proper checks and surveillance. We're starved of spare parts that we need. You know we have to make them ourselves, some of them. We broke down on the way out and it could happen again.'

It did.

I was on the 1200 to 1600 hours watch when the *Venetia*'s movements became more violent. The comforting vibrations of running engines ceased and I heard raised voices outside the cabin. Mr Michaels and the chief engineer were having a set to. Smith came into the radio cabin and said;

'We've put up the black balls. The commodore has signalled that the convoy will slow and could we speed repairs.' He added wryly, 'that's the one good thing about our cargo. Its safety definitely has a high priority.'

I nipped out on deck in time to see the lines of the convoy showing us clear water. It was an ugly moment. The mate doubled lookouts and the two marines stood by their gun. We felt very vulnerable and alone. The heroes that day were the engineers; they all worked down below like demented beavers. They were fuelled on a supply of sandwiches and cocoa, of which an endless supply was sent down to them. I returned to the radio cabin and took back my watch.

'Are you frightened?' asked Smith, surprisingly.

'Well ... I'm not madly happy.' He smiled.

'There's a very thin line between being a coward and being realistic. Anyway, should anything happen just be quick off the mark. Get out the transmission three times, slowly and clearly, and then get to your boat station. Now, voice tube the bridge and get an update on our exact position.'

Four hours after we had broken down we were underway again. The engineers were the toast of the ship. The chief engineer called on Mr Michaels and presented him with a list of spares and replacements that he needed as soon as we reached a home port. The captain said that he would pass the list onto the company's agent but doubted that the chief would get all he requisitioned, what with the war and the shortages and all that. The chief huffed that in that case he would not sail on the *Venetia* again and he would advise his staff to find different ships. This led to inevitable acrimony between the pair, but it was ameliorated by Stevey's constant topping up of the engineer's glass with brandy. As Stevey observed, the chief was partial to good Reny Martin, especially that belonging to other people. The Old Man assured him that he would stress the importance of the list to the company, and this, together with the brandy and corned beef sandwiches, mollified the chief. Then Mr Michaels asked him to increase speed to nine knots until we caught up with the convoy. At that the chief's good humour seeped away and he exploded;

'Do you want us to spend another four hours of frantic make-do down in that hell hole? We're nursing the bloody engines when we're just ticking over!'

Nevertheless he did increase revolutions and as darkness fell we were relieved to sight the convoy ahead. As we steamed up the columns to take up our station the feeling of welcome home from the other ships could almost be felt. When I went on watch at 2000 hours I quickly received a position from the mate. It was longitude 32 west and a latitude just north of John O'Groats. The convoy was making heavy going through gale force winds and spiteful seas so when Smith relieved me at midnight I hesitated about going forward to see Pablo. But he was expecting me, so I went, keeping tightly hold of the lifeline. Smith and the Old Man would not have approved but I enjoyed playing chess and was hooked on learning Spanish. The spray soaked me but after the stuffy heat of the radio cabin it was wonderfully astringent.

The next morning three ships left the convoy, the *Empire Unity*, the *Chesapeake* and the *J. W. McKnight*. Once they had fallen back well clear of the convoy they headed on a north-westerly course. Our AMC signalled good luck to us all and fell back to join them. We watched her go with dismay and anger. The three ships carried a range of cargoes and speculation had it that they were taking supplies to our forces in Iceland. Our commodore signalled us to close up and maintain set course. Later that afternoon our grumbles were stifled by the approach of a destroyer, a very comforting sight. Chippy said that exchanging an AMC for a destroyer was like losing a penny and finding a shilling. Within two hours we saw the dots and smoke puffs of many ships on the horizon ahead. We were combining with another convoy.

The following day some of us tried to count the ships we had joined. Estimates varied between eighteen and twenty-four, but we never did know for certain. The mate informed us that two convoys had left Halifax in Nova Scotia and Sydney, Cape Breton Island, and had joined up south of Newfoundland. It was this one large convoy that we had joined. What satisfied us was the naval escort; it comprised two destroyers sheep-dogging the flanks of the convoy, an AMC smack in the middle and a frigate that tailed the convoy and would act as a rescue vessel to pick up survivors from sunken ships. The large number of ships, fully laden, made us an important convoy for the Royal Navy to protect and the Kriegsmarine to sink.

Aboard the *Venetia* the minutiae of everyday life helped to fill the off-watch periods. My hair had grown long and curly and beyond the control of comb and brush. I mentioned this to Stevey, who offered to cut it. I laughed;

'Don't say you've been a barber as well!'

I could have guessed the confident reply. He claimed to be a dab hand with scissors and had worked for nine months in a barber's saloon in Manchester. I crossed my fingers and let him have his way. It was a surprisingly credible haircut and Roy turned me round and round in the saloon.

'The old bugger hasn't made a bad job of it, and he's still left the ears on your head,' he exclaimed. As a result Stevey did Roy, Johnny, Ian and the mate. News of his prowess spread and he cut the hair of the engineers, the bosun, Chippy and the two marines. 'Is there anything that man cannot do?' wondered Roy.

Having carefully packed a tea chest filled with his model animals, Chippy had turned to carving birds. He worked from a coffee table compendium that had full page illustrations of all the different species in detail. Smith had become very engrossed in his delicate blueprint. I had only been inside his cabin twice during the entire trip and had seen his impressive collection of technical books on electrical circuits. I was sure he was inventing or improving something, but when I ventured to say that what he was doing looked interesting, he just smiled and agreed. Johnny and Ian spent long periods studying for their certificates and Wilkie asked me to get him books from the saloon library. It was not the done thing, but I did it. He always returned the books very quickly, with thanks.

Our 600 metres reception kept us aware of the predators after our blood. Seventy miles to the south a lone ship was torpedoed. A German Focke-Wulf bombed a merchantman off Pentland Firth. A U-boat surfaced and shelled an independent tanker en route to the west. A wolf pack mauled a convoy some 130 miles to the south-east. Smith recorded four SSSS calls. East of 30 degrees west and we entered U-boat alley for a second time. It was as psychologically traumatic as crossing a hostile frontier. That same day Mr Michaels made a rare appearance in the saloon for lunch. I was on watch but Johnny gave me the details. Apparently the captain was in a loquacious mood, rambling on about how war changed peacetime values. When a ship foundered in peacetime the top priority was saving lives, whereas in wartime the worth of everything depended up its usefulness and ease of replacement. Hence, he concluded, the *Venetia* was more important than its company.

'And that,' piped up the irrepressible Roy, 'is what really worries Mrs Garrett's son.'

Even Mr Michaels managed a fearsome smile at the sally. Then he got down to the reason for his presence, the passing on of information.

'From now onwards,' he said, 'the chances of us being attacked are high. Convoys do get through without incident, and if we do, that's all well and good. If not, here are the instructions issued at the Bermuda captains' conference. If just one or two ships are picked off the convoy will close ranks to give the escorts a smaller area to protect.'

The mate interjected that closing up was a dangerous procedure.

'Aye, Mr Parkinson, it is,' Mr Michaels replied. 'Especially in high seas and bad visibility and with some of the ships badly in need of engine overhauling. However, if we are hit by a large pack and they come between the convoy lanes and ships are going down in large numbers our orders are to scatter immediately. I have decided that the *Venetia* will head due north for twenty-four hours. You can pray or keep your fingers crossed, or both ...' The heavy humour went down like the proverbial lead balloon. Mr Michaels continued. 'In this event the RAF coastal command will send out flying boats to search for survivors. If one of them spots us it will give us a course to follow which will lead us to other survivors. A strong naval escort will take us into the Clyde. Any questions?'

'What happens if the RAF don't find us?' asked Roy.

'In that eventually we turn and head flat out for the Clyde.'

'Shit or bust?' murmured the mate.

'Exactly so, Mr Parkinson. We will increase lookouts with one permanently on monkey-island with binoculars. The gun crew must be ready to spring into instant action and anyone seen without their lifejacket to hand will be in deep trouble with me.' He added a final order. 'The lifeboat lockers must be checked to see that they have the regulation quantities of drinking water, brandy and ships biscuits.'

Nearing Iceland, black, low clouds turned noon into dusk. Sleet stabbed down and a head-on swell reduced the convoy's speed. Ships were struggling to maintain station and we had slowed to a painful crawl. Weighed down by her cargo, the *Venetia* cleaved through the onrushing walls of water like a cyclist with his head bowed. Torrents of water washed over the well-deck and hands working on it lashed themselves to the handiest iron protuberance. Life became clammy and miserable and we all longed for hot food and dryness.

A freak wave smashed in one of the focsle ventilator covers on the focsle head and water poured through, soaking bunks, clothing, baggage and sleeping men. The bosun and a seaman tied themselves to the ventilator while they fitted a new cover. The focsle was always dank and smelled of wet wool, but with mattresses soaked and blankets hopelessly damp it became too much to bear. The bosun went aft and had words with the chief engineer. As a result the affected hands took their wet bedclothes down into the engine room and spread them out. By the end of the day they were dry as a bone. The mate had a knack of doing the right thing at the right time. He called the bosun and the seaman who had helped him to repair the cover to his cabin and gave each a large tot of brandy. Bronchitis bunked a greaser and colds and chills affected everyone as eyes reddened, noses streamed and working was accompanied by helpful non-stop cursing. We all thought nostalgically of the Caribbean warmth.

The central heating in the radio cabin comprised a five-inch diameter pipe which fitted into the join where the deck met the long inner bulkhead. Two hours into my noon watch a join cracked and exploded into a spray of painful stifling steam. In a moment it had turned the cabin into a Turkish bath. Reception became impossible so I voice-tubed up to Roy. I must have sounded frantic.

'I need help, Urgently. Steam pipe has burst. The radio log is soaked and so am I. Reception is hopeless. I've had to cover the receiver with my jacket to protect it. Could get a short somewhere vital ...'

Roy was good. Straightaway he realised the predicament.

'I'll get onto the engineers right away. Can you cover the leak with a cloth? No? I'll send the lookout down with some thick canvas. Meanwhile switch off all lights. Pull your blackout curtain right across the door. Open it and step out for a breather.'

Within a few minutes I had the canvas, folded over and re-doubled into four thicknesses. With the lookout's help I jammed it over the fracture and with the aid of a large screwdriver got it between the bulkhead and the pipe and underneath between the deck and the pipe.

'Thanks, Dave,' I said to the lookout.

'You're bloody soaking. Want me to go to your cabin and get a towel and a dry vest and shirt?' I nodded. He cleared it with Roy and got me my things. Then Arne Rolleson the Dane came in with his toolbag. He lifted a small wooden cover over the end of the pipe and forced a valve anti-clockwise as far as it would go. He took off the canvas to reveal that the gout of steam had reduced to just a tiny trickle of water.

'It needs a new join, I think,' he said. 'Be done tomorrow, Sparky.'

I chilled rapidly but using the towel I mopped up as best I could, concentrating on removing moisture from the equipment. When Smith took over I was very tired. I told him what had happened and he told me to get below and dry properly and get a good sleep. He did not want me to get any indispositions that would affect my ability to work properly. Out on deck I saw that the well-deck seemed so low under water that we could have silhouetted like a submarine. Each time we rose on a crest I could see other ships making heavy going of it. In my cabin I just flopped on my bunk. I lay there with my neck-breaker clutched on my chest, listening to the gurgling and hissing of my radiator, and fell fast asleep, missing lunch.

A sixth sense awoke me, like a mouse sensing a cat close by. I sat up and pricked my ears and yes, the siren was blowing those stomach-churning blasts. I urged myself to move. Move. Get up. Put on your shoes, jacket, coat, scarf ... now bloody move yourself!

Into the alleyway. It was deserted. I could hear the sirens more clearly. I stepped over the stormboard onto the well-deck and icy waters slopped over my shoes and soaked my socks and trouser bottoms. It was getting dark and a straggly line of bemused men were emerging from the focsle and making their way along the flybridge to the boat stations. Their lifejackets made them look very bulky as they swayed to the motion of the ship. I went up to the radio cabin and could see that Smith had been busily drying the log book with sheets of blotting paper. Apparently Stevey had told him that I was so deeply asleep when he came to wake me for lunch that he didn't have the heart to rouse me. For that Smith rebuked me, saying that no matter how bad the food was I had to eat it in order to work efficiently. He had picked up one SSSS call from a Bristolian on our convoy.

'Just one?' I asked. Smith nodded. In my ignorance I added, 'well, that's not so bad.'

'It couldn't be worse,' replied Smith. 'It means that at this very moment our convoy is a juicy topic of conversation between operational U-boats between our position and home. Trouble has found us. Go to your boat station and from now onwards I'm giving you an order which you must never break. It only takes one of us to transmit an SSSS so if I'm on watch when it happens don't come here but go straight to your boat station.'

Out on deck I heard the explosion of depth charges away to the starboard rear of the convoy. My boat station companions were different to when we had mustered here on the way out. Then, we were empty, in ballast. Now we were sitting on tanks loaded with high octane fuel and we all knew that between the top of the liquid and the tank covers were cavities filled with the most inflammable fumes. The men were silent, morose and afraid. They were not cowards, far from it. During my years with the Merchant Navy and afterwards I heard many stories and even met participants in acts of bravery by merchant seamen which in the armed forces would have merited recognition by a medal. Giving up their places in an overcrowded and waterlogged lifeboat and slipping into icy waters to die; going back on sinking ships to rescue trapped comrades; and maintaining morale and discipline during long days in lifeboats. Being a civilian service its men won civilian decorations like the OBE and MBE and not too many of those. Not that it mattered to the merchant seamen. The matters of import to them were their pay, the food and the living conditions. Their pay for the work they did and the hours they put in was paltry. The National Union of Seamen could not improve it, and demanding extra pay was regarded as unpatriotic. No, they were not cowards, but they were silent because they knew enough about war at sea to know that for the U-boats the single snatched victim was the aperitif before the main meal to come. Johnny sidled up to me and slipped a stick of chewing gum into my hand.

'Got it in Aruba. Kept it for something like this. Chew it otherwise we won't hear the torpedo strike through your teeth chattering.'

More depth charge explosions. The night had become clear and very starry. I realised I would get no sleep before my 0800 hours watch. Yet I felt completely awake. More depth charges. We never knew whether the navy had made contact or were trying to frighten off the attackers. Stevey appeared and said;

'Brew up. Tea in the pantry.'

'Does Twitch know?' asked Johnny.

'He's too busy stuffing bank notes into his moneybag to worry about anything else.'

We repaired to my cabin and munched toast and drank tea. If Smith had seen me away from the boat-deck he would have been very displeased, but what the hell. The feeling was that the attack was over. The U-boat commander had done his work. He had successfully trailed the convoy and had claimed a victim. That must be worth an Iron Cross, observed Stevey. Johnny asked Stevey when he had been in the Germany navy. Stevey had to think hard about that one.

At a latitude level with the Faroe Islands the convoy reached its northern limit and swung due east. We crossed longitude 20 west. The ships closed ranks uncomfortably near to one another and we saw more of the guarding destroyers. We were all vigilant and watchful. We ploughed through violent weather and they were arduous days but there was no attack. Waiting for the expected was the hardest thing to bear.

It was at this point that an elderly freighter put up the black balls and fell out. Watching her wallowing and tossed helplessly by the strength of the angry seas as she fell behind us made me sympathise with her engineers, no doubt working frantically down below to get her moving again. We thought of our own two bouts of engine trouble and crossed our fingers. A destroyer dropped back to circle round her. They exchanged aldis lamp signals and then the destroyer returned to us.

'She's a goner,' said Stevey as he served us in the saloon.

'Not necessarily,' corrected the mate. 'Our stalker is concentrating on the convoy, so there's a chance she's fallen back unnoticed. Still, I wouldn't like to be in her shoes.'

'Supposing the damage is so irreparable that she can't get going again? What then?' I asked.

'Then,' said the mate, 'she could founder and go down. A lot depends on what she's carrying. In that case the crew will abandon ship and take to the boats and Sparks will send out SOS distress calls and hope to pick up a response.' He added thoughtfully, 'they could make the Faroes in the boats. It would be a rough trip, but they could do it.'

At longitude 17 degrees west the commodore ship raised a signal which pleased no one. It was to the effect that henceforth there would be no slowing of convoy speed to allow stragglers to catch up. Ships which broke down would have to take their chances. The *Venetia*'s crew remembered our own breakdowns and the superstitious spat three times into the wind and caressed rabbits' feet and determined to stay ashore if they ever reached it. Yet, as we ploughed eastwards across the roof of the Atlantic everything seemed so unwarlike, even peaceful. The men played board games, wrote letters and yarned. Their talk, as so often, turned to food. It was strange how the demands of empty stomachs pushed fear into the background.

On Friday 20 September there was heavy rain and visibility dropped to a few yards. The blowing of whistles and tolling of bells revealed several maverick captains who were more afraid of collision than breaking the ban on carrying noises. It was eerie and unnerving hearing and not seeing the ships around us. It was 1100 hours ship's time when a tall-masted stranger was spotted close astern. There she stayed, sometimes edging closer, sometimes falling back. A destroyer fell astern, placing herself between the stranger and the convoy. There was no way at this stage that any of our escorts would leave their close protection of the convoy. In the late afternoon the strange ship disappeared from sight and never re-appeared.

'I bet it was a bloody neutral, Swede or Finn,' said the bosun. 'Don't trust the bloody Finns. If Jerry didn't know our position before he'll know it now, and our course and escort.'

I had a quickly taken desultory lunch with Ian and Roy in the saloon. No one was in the mood to converse. Even Stevey was unusually lugubrious and taciturn. When I went out on deck for a quick breather I found that the rain had stopped; the wind had fallen but there was a low-hanging and frustrating mist. I was now picking up the first enemy 'blue blue blue' calls from British coastal stations. Smith had recorded SSSS calls 250 miles away to the south-west. Ian voice-tubed down and gave me our position, and reported that there were bangs in the distance. It could have been gunfire but he was not certain. That same afternoon the SS *Invershannon* and five other ships left us. They were escorted by a destroyer and a sloop that had joined us only a few hours earlier, thus dashing our joy at what we had thought was a happy addition to our own escorts. Ian said that they were peeling off to Scapa Flow while the rest of us were heading for the Scottish west coast, probably the Clyde.

That same day, while I was on my afternoon watch, there was much manoeuvring in the convoy as ships were allotted new stations by the commodore. We found ourselves the fourth ship down the middle column. There were now five columns with six ships in each column. This placed the *Venetia* in a more comfortable position, but no one could fathom the reason for the changes although none of the seven tankers, including ourselves, was in an outside lane. A merchant seaman on his ship in convoy was in an analogous situation to an infantryman in his slit trench in the forefront of battle. Just as the soldier knew very little about the scheme of things that put him where he was, so the merchant seaman's vision was confined to his ship.

Dinner was a terrible affair, a lukewarm stew of god-knows-what, but the mate, Ian and I ate mechanically. After Smith relieved me at 2400 hours he told me to turn in and get some sleep, and that it was an order. His manner convinced me that he knew about my nocturnal visits to Pablo. He said that after breakfast I had to check the specific gravity of the battery cells and the terminal fastenings. I lay in my bunk, too wound-up to sleep. Through a chink in the blackout paint on my porthole I watched stars swing in and out of vision. There was a violent coughing from the chief steward, a heavy smoker. He could not stop the wracking explosions. Roy called out:

'Jesus bloody Christ hurry up and die. I can't sleep.'

'Bleeding Aussie … bugger off back to Australia.'

Distant explosions. I placed my towel over my head, trying to muffle all sounds. It was hopeless. I picked up my torch and a book and read, staring at the words without taking them in.

9

AMBUSH

At longitude 13 degrees west the convoy altered course to almost due south. It was the run-in to a home port. The commodore ordered an increase of speed by one knot. This evoked a further protest from our chief engineer at the strain put on the clapped-out engines but the increase stood. We were like revellers trying to sneak home before the milk is delivered and the wives are awake. There was a sharp tang of Blighty in the air as the crew set about making parcels for wives and girlfriends. We packed our sugar bags into made-to-measure crates knocked up by Chippy. Go-ashores were cleaned and repaired and sheltered corners had their fill of rigged-up washing. A feeling of good cheer spread from ship to ship. The one malignant shadow was the Luftwaffe's bombing of Britain. The more we thought about it the worse we imagined its effects, especially those of us who lived in London. A persistent worry that we would go home to bad news nagged at our hearts. The fact that millions were in the same boat was no help.

On Saturday 21 September 1940 we were still steaming southwards. Winds had dropped and the seas had moderated. Staring across the water we could see most of the ships and none appeared to be struggling. At breakfast Stevey said knowingly:

'That was gunfire last night. Definitely.'

'Oh yes,' Roy raised his eyebrows. 'German or ours? What type of guns? And, my dear professor on every subject, what calibre were the shells?'

'Aussie idiot,' retorted Stevey. Roy grinned. But the galley wireless had it that the stranger which had tagged us for hours was an armed raider and had been seen off duly by one of our destroyers. The galley was seldom without its quota of off-duty seamen and greasers seeking cups of tea or cocoa and the odd sandwich or sausage. They gossiped and nothing went on in the ship that they did not know about. There were two taboo topics: the cargo and the U-boats that were certainly homing in. Everyone carried his neck-breaker.

After breakfast I went up to monkey-island and checked over the batteries, their terminals and the insulators. It was a glorious day with the sun breaking through the clouds. The lookout was an able seaman named Jean Callau, a French-Canadian born in Quebec. He was in his mid-twenties, swarthy with an athletic build. He gave me the binoculars to look through and I swept the seas wondering if I would even notice a U-boat's periscope. Callou had the same thought. He was looking forward to seeing his girlfriend in South Shields. I finished off my work by dipping my hands into a tin of that foul black grease and protectively smothering the terminals with it.

My noon watch passed smoothly with GBR banging out its coded messages to ships everywhere. There were two 'blue blue blue' warnings from coastal transmitters and I wondered which cities and towns were going to cop it. When Smith relieved me at 1600 hours ship's time he carried a waterproofed roll about five inches in diameter. He was in a taciturn mood.

'Your work?' I ventured bravely. He nodded and added cautiously that after the war he was going ashore to manufacture a new concept in powerful miniature receivers. Then he clammed up and told me to hop it. After a blow on deck I went down to my cabin, tried to sleep and failed. Sleep was in short supply. Johnny came in and talked, and

Stevey, hearing us, brought us two mugs of tea. He asked whether we would like some corned beef sandwiches. Would we? Not half.

We chatted and ate and then they left. I flopped back on my bunk and fell into a half sleep in which I dreamt vividly of home, the cosiness of the large lounge with its open fire, my two sisters exclaiming over my gift of Bermudan sugar. I was conscious of a siren shrieking out short blasts. Spray pattered, the seas murmured and the wind whooshed and then the mate banged on my door and shouted;

'Move, quickly! To your boat station!' Johnny burst in, pulled me upright and gasped,

'Come on, Sparky, it's the big one.' Then he was gone, careful to put my door on the latch.

The *Venetia* shuddered as she slew violently to starboard. My glass tumbler fell into the sink and shattered. Then I heard a prolonged booming as if oil drums were falling from a great height onto a corrugated tin roof. I knew it was another torpedoing. The short blasts continued, communicating alert, alarm, fear. The chief steward ran past, shouting as he went. He went through the blackout curtains at the alleyway entrance and the wind smothered his voice. Through scratches in the blackout paint on my porthole I glimpsed streaks of red fire. Stevey appeared.

'Come on, you slow bugger. Get out of here.' He lit a cigarette, handed it to me and said, 'have a couple of deep drags. They'll steady you.' At that moment a nearby ship was hammered. Her explosion was loud and the blast made the *Venetia* tremor. 'The old girl's got the wind up and so have I.' He grabbed my arms and pulled me into the alleyway and out onto the sloping well-deck.

The U-boat pack had set its ambush well. The wolves had leapt at their prey with a vengeance and during that misty northern night a furious one-sided action was being waged. In the middle of it all the *Venetia* turned and twisted as she headed northwards trying to get clear of the perimeter of the spreading battle to escape the lethal enemies she could not see. Mr Michaels, the mate and Roy were all on the upper bridge. Ian was in charge of the starboard boat station and Johnny was with me on the port muster station. Should the *Venetia* be hit and the upper bridge wiped out then the acting third mate and the apprentice would be in charge of their respective boats. Johnny stood beside me.

'They bounced up without being spotted. They came up right between the convoy lanes. Everyone dispersed immediately, each for himself ...' his flow was stopped by the torpedoing of a ship carrying a deck cargo of British Columbian timber. She had been cutting across our stern about half a mile away when she was hit. We heard the explosion, felt the blast and saw flickers of flame beneath her funnel. A destroyer raced to where she was listing badly and dropped depth charge patterns.

I later learned that the first victim, a Dutchman, cargo unknown, was hit at 1900 hours. The torpedo strike started a conflagration which took hold slowly and then picked up a remorseless momentum which engulfed the entire ship. The survivors managed to get two boats away. The next victim was the *Turinco*, followed by the *Broompark* and the *Collegian*. The darkening evening presented an astonishingly beautiful and terrible picture. Torpedoes struck home, ships were burning, guns barked. At what? What could they see? Were surfaced U-boats shelling ships? The destroyers were racing pell-mell to the scenes of action and dropping depth charges. Had they made contact? Sirens sounded. Here and there distress rockets showered red balls of fire which all too quickly dissolved into nothing. White parachute flares hovered gently between the low cloud and the gently swelling ocean, and U-boats kept firing them to illuminate the area. There were burning ships and phantom ships steaming flat out. A destroyer tore past us perilously close like a police car after getaway villains. As we watched, another ship burst into flame about two-and-a-half miles on our starboard quarter. Roy came down to address us all on the boat-deck.

'The Old Man has ordered me to tell you that we shall be maintaining a northerly course. The submarines will be hunting for victims, especially since we're homeward bound with full cargoes. So those off-watch must stay mustered by their boats. Maltese Johnny, Einstein and Stevey will be making tea, cocoa and sandwiches for as long as the emergency lasts. He's in a nervous state so we don't want him overwhelmed; everyone is to go down in pairs. The first pair can go now … No!' shouted Roy, as every man on the boat-deck made a move. 'Just two at a time. Okay? Got it?'

Mandel the Pole and Cockney Collins were the first to go. Suddenly we were all startled by a shout.

'Look, look!' It was Ginger. He was pointing frantically down at the sea at a small boat, probably a jolly boat, capsized and no more than twenty yards from us. Three men sprawled across its beam, hanging on, their faces white blobs. They were shouting at us but none could decipher what they were saying and in a flash we were past them. We felt very ashamed but there was nothing we could do. We knew that unless they were very lucky they would soon be dead. Roy muttered a heartfelt curse and then went round to the starboard boat-deck. The *Venetia* rose and fell and slipped and wallowed and we passed through the stench of burning oil.

'Remember the Norwegian tanker next to us when we left Bermuda?' asked Johnny. 'That's what you're smelling.'

I sighted along his pointing arm and saw the red flaming mass with its billowing column of thick black smoke. Even at four miles distance it was an awesome sight. On that wet, cold, miserable boat-deck we stood, leaned and squatted, all eyes and ears, senses sharpened by fear. Our benighted cargo was very much on our minds but a calming smoke was out of the question. Attempts at laboured humour irritated, living as we did at the whim of a U-boat captain.

Bravado dared not raise its hypocritical head; we were all afraid and unashamed about showing it. Many had been shipwrecked before and knew what they might face, and so talk died away and each man hunched into himself, keeping his thoughts and feelings to himself.

The rain increased to a mild downpour. Another growling detonation was borne on the wind and some two miles to port another torpedoed merchantman was etched against the night as it fed an enlarging fire, an animal dying in its own spreading blood. The mate voice-tubed down to the engine room and pleaded for more speed. He spoke to the second engineer, Ernie Charlton from Sunderland. Ernie's reply was blunt.

'Forget it.'

'Try, Ernie. The best you can ...'

'I'm not playing games down here. If I could, I would. But the chief has stipulated the maximum revolutions beyond which we must not go.'

The mate sighed and replaced the voice tube, banging the plug back into it. Mr Michaels shook his head and cursed the engineers for always causing problems. The mate and Roy exchanged looks, both smiled and looked skywards.

Despite Smith's instructions to stay on the boat-deck until my watch I went to the radio cabin at 2030 hours. Smith was distracted and weary, but not so much that he could not snap at me at me to go back to my station. I insisted that I should do my watch and he unbent and sighed.

'Come back in half an hour.'

'How many?'

'Six ... so far that I've picked up. There may be more. As we'll be in an area of escaping ships and hunting U-boats with their tails up for some hours I'm sure there'll be more. Just hope we're not one of them.'

Back on the boat-deck the wind seemed to have gotten stronger, perhaps because we were all tired and damp.

'I don't mind being torpedoed but not when it's raining,' brought the first genuine laugh of the day. Then three miles astern a ship was hit. The violent explosion flash was soon swallowed by the night. She did not burn. More depth charges seemed to tear holes in the earth itself, their shock waves being strong enough to kill nearby swimmers. All through that long drawn-out attack the engine room staff worked in a state of utmost trepidation well below the waterline as they waited for a torpedo to burst through. Theirs was the worst and most dangerous situation of all of us. I went to relieve Smith.

'Any more?'

'Two. One very close and the other quite a way off.'

Without another word he left me to it. The radio cabin was stifling hot. The steam heat was full on. I took off my neck-breaker, coat and jacket, and yet still I perspired. Smith had filled two full pages of the log with entries, the first time it had happened in one watch. Just a short while ago home had seemed so close, but now ...

While I sweated in the cabin the marines on the gun deck maintained a most uncomfortable vigil. A phone line linked them to the wheelhouse. They were bursting with eagerness to open fire at anything but could only do so with the permission of the deck officer on duty. Maltese Johnny, Einstein and Stevey kept the drinks and sandwiches going for the men on the boat-deck, a heroic effort. The Old Man steered the ship in zig-zags. Like the other surviving merchantmen we had no idea where our busy escorts were, although faint explosions could be heard from time to time. For a while we ran parallel with another ship half a mile off our starboard beam, but Mr Michaels abruptly diverged away from it westwards; there was no point giving a U-boat two sitting ducks.

Slowly the explosions grew fainter and fewer in number. Then there were none, no more fireballs, flames or flickers. No more parachute flares lighting up all beneath them. Faces were gaunt, hollow-cheeked and creased with fatigue. Wilkie meditatively chewed an unlit cigarette between his powerful jaws. The bosun, a squat pyramid beneath his outer oilskins, looked morosely dependable. The chief steward sat by himself, his head bowed into his chest and clutching a waterproofed case. Lookouts were being changed every two hours, and now that the heavy hand of danger seemed to have lifted, many, overwhelmed by physical fatigue and mental strain, only wanted to retire to their bunks. They reckoned that over the four hours since the start of the attack the *Venetia* had covered thirty-five miles and surely that was distance enough. The mate came down to the boat-deck and explained that if the *Venetia* could travel that distance then so could a U-boat, and he had barely stopped talking when another ship was torpedoed two miles to port. It was too close for comfort and the mutinous torpor by the boats gave way to a terrible disappointment. The men stared angrily at the showers of red sparks shooting skywards from the funnel of the stricken ship as the *Venetia* abruptly changed course once again.

'Sorry lads,' said the mate, 'the emergency stays and if the worst happens don't wait for orders from the bridge. Just get that boat into the water pronto and yourselves into it.'

At 2232 I recorded that torpedoing. Everyone was wide awake now, but weariness made them see torpedo wakes and steel cigars breaking the surface of the sea everywhere. The marine sergeant phoned through to the wheelhouse and reported a sighting. Mr Michaels answered.

'How certain are you?'

'Pretty certain, sir,' he said hopefully.

'Not good enough, sergeant. Do not open fire.'

Dot on midnight Smith came into the cabin. I protested that I could do a bit longer; he looked very tired and rough around the edges. He had not slept. He told me to go back to the boat-deck and to have faith in Mr Michaels' judgement over ending the emergency. He asked if I had had cocoa and sandwiches while on watch, and I replied that I had not.

136

'That's a bad omission, I'll take that up later. Before you go to the boat-deck go to the galley and get your share. It's as vital as sleep.'

It was five hours into the emergency. The ship's bell was silenced for the change of watches because sound carries so far at sea. Men changed over silently. Harry Reed, the third engineer, came up from down below, wearing a coat over his dungarees. He was edgy and completely drained from mental and physical effort. He sat down with his back against a bulkhead, placing his hands on outstretched legs and closed his eyes.

'Howie, I'm completely knackered. The engine room was like a bloody sounding box.' In an instant he fell asleep.

By 0100 hours on Sunday 22 September 1940 our position was longitude 11.44 west and latitude 55.59 north. The rain had ceased. Stern up, stern down; roll to port and back again. Scattered groups of stars twinkled and the frightened moon slipped from behind the clouds and glinted silvery off the wave tops. Conversation had just about died away completely.

'I'd give my arm for a smoke.'

'Someone should invent a blackout fag.'

I fell asleep on my feet, wedged between a ventilator and a bulkhead. A heavy lurch wakened me. The men around me were lost in a kind of wakeful coma, their faces taut with strain. Two were down on the well-deck clutching the rail, talking intensely, seemingly unaware of how soaked they were getting. Wilkie still chewed an unlit cigarette, the bosun catnapped on a coil of rope, and up in the wheelhouse Mr Michaels lay stretched out on a settee-cum-bed. Derek Kenny, the Welsh able seaman, held the spokes of the wheel and stared woodenly at the compass. The mate and Roy paced to and from the starboard wing of the bridge, quietly conversing. Long John and Cockney Collins were lookouts on monkey-island.

Occasionally the members of the gun crew visited the galley for cocoa, rolling the enamel tin mugs over their chilled noses, ears and cheeks before drinking. I visited the radio cabin, only to find Smith in an amiable, even light-hearted mood.

'You know,' he said, 'the Muslims have got it right with their fatalistic approach to life. What will happen will happen ...' Then he became sombre. 'By God, we've taken a pasting tonight.'

At 0300 hours ship's time the mate ambled down to the boat-deck and told everyone the emergency was over, but that everyone had to sleep fully clothed. I watched the seamen and greasers shamble back along the flybridge liked a humped elongated caterpillar, muscling itself back into the focsle. I fell into my bunk and in no time at all a lookout was shaking me and saying that I was on watch in five minutes. On deck for a quick breather. We had the sea to ourselves, the first time since we had left Bermuda, and we were heading due south. Blighty or bust – Mr Michaels was adhering to his programme. Feelings about him had changed; from being a tyrannical old shellback he was now a captain who inspired confidence. Back in the radio cabin a cockroach raced over the logbook and stopped.

'Cheeky sod,' I murmured, and shook it onto the deck. I refrained from squashing it. 'Join the club. If we burn, so will you.'

At 0530 hours our marines saw gun flashes about three miles off our starboard quarter. A merchantman was being shelled by a U-boat, and was replying with its pop gun aft. Mr Michaels ordered another state of emergency and the word was passed from man to man throughout the ship. The *Venetia* changed to a course directly away from the gunfight and the disappointed gun crew were denied their chance to open fire. The radio officers on the beleaguered vessel managed to get out their distress call three times in copybook measured Morse code giving position and the fact that they were being shelled. This useful information told the collators of intelligence on shore that if one U-boat had used up its torpedoes then almost certainly others would have done likewise. If no German milk cow submarine was around to restock them they would have to head back to their French coastal bases. Perhaps, on their way back, the Royal Navy, aided by the RAF coastal command, could bounce them.

It was around the middle of my watch that I was suddenly affected by a delayed shock of fear. It struck me hard how lucky we were to have escaped and, more to the point, that we were not home yet. I became ultra alert to every sound; a clanging of metal nearby had me leaping to my feet. Thank God I could confess to Johnny how I felt, and to my relief he said that everyone suffered the same thoughts and fears, but no one would admit to it. When I told avuncular Chippy, a man with whom I felt totally at ease, he said:

'Those who claim they have no fear either have a block of wood filling their brain cavity or are bloody liars. We've been lucky. They go for tankers, especially loaded ones.' He patted my shoulder and said, 'we're not home yet by a long chalk, but we'll get home. I feel it in my guts.'

The watch did not lack for interest. A merchantman issued an SSSS some sixty miles south-west. She was being abandoned by her crew. I voice-tubed up to Roy.

'Good news, Sparky,' he said cheerfully. 'Two hours ago we were spotted by a Sunderland flying boat. She gave us a course to follow and right now through my binoculars I can see ships and a destroyer just on the horizon ahead. We'll soon have company again.'

At 0800 hours Smith took over. His powers of resilience were admirable; he was back to his normal alert and sartorially immaculate self, down to his pristine white collar and ironed black tie under a long-sleeved navy sweater. He ordered me to go down for breakfast and then to sleep, but out on deck I could not help but linger. A coastal command plane was making slow wide circles overhead. The yellowish sun cleared the horizon and there was a moderate wind, but visibility was good. When I went down to my cabin to wash and comb my hair, Stevey bustled in on my heels.

'The Old Man's down at breakfast,' he warned. 'He sent Johnny packing to put on his blues, though Roy got away with his tunic jacket over his sweater. He'll chew you to pieces if you don't put on the works.'

'Oh God.' I swore and changed. The breakfast comprised a sort of porridge, which I think even Oliver Twist would have turned his nose up at, and bread, butter and jam. Mr Michaels sensed our unspoken disgust and said firmly;

'The cook and his boy have had two very sleepless hard nights. They have done well.'

'No one can argue with that, sir,' sighed Roy.

After breakfast I fell into such a deep sleep that I could hardly be awakened. Out on deck I saw that we were one of seven merchantmen with a destroyer and sloop as escort. We steamed in a convoy of two columns with three ships in one and four in the other. We were the fourth on the starboard column. There was incessant coastal command activity as planes rounded up stray ships and kept an eye out for the enemy. During my noon watch we joined five more survivors and formed up into a convoy of twelve ships, three in each column, our position being the third ship in the third column counting from the port side. We now had an escort of three destroyers and the sloop, which reflected Winston Churchill's concern over heavy Merchant Navy losses. All possible resources were being mobilised to get us home safely, and right up to darkness planes were always in sight. Before going to my 0800 hours watch I went up to the wheelhouse to gaze across the convoy. We were closed up with the destroyers each guarding a flank and the sloop at the tail. We were racing southwards for the Minches and the Clyde. The mate, puffing his pipe, came to stand alongside me and asked how I like being at sea.

'It's interesting because it's all new to me, sir. Things can be monotonous and then all sorts of things erupt.'

'They do, laddie. And when we get to the Clyde things could well erupt. And, if that happens, whatever it is, you heed Mr Smith's advice and keep well out of things.' Food for thought. The mate was a serious man. Night brought a stark worsening of weather and by 2000 hours the gale had whipped up to force eight. It howled through the rigging, seeped icy draughts through chinks, down ventilators and through latched doors. High waves howled across the well-deck and rain mixed with spray lashed the ship. Low cloud masses virtually blotted out the moon and stars and visibility fell sharply. Progress became possible only along the flybridge exposed to the wind, the rain and continuous gouts of spray.

That night we lost Cockney Collins. He had finished his lookout on monkey-island at midnight and had been relieved by Jean Callou. After the usual exchange of pleasantries Callou huddled into his favourite corner where he could escape exposure to the worst of the elements from his chest downwards, and Collins made his way down to the flybridge. He never reached the focsle, but was not missed for four hours until the next watch changeover. Mandel and Long John saw Collins was not in his bunk as she should have been, and furthermore his blankets and waterproof coverings were as he had left them before his watch. Alarmed, they checked the lavatories and the shower booths, but with no success. Their efforts aroused others in the focsle. Perils at sea attuned seamen to the fact that when a shipmate was in trouble, action rather than words were priority. Wilkie shot out of his bunk and started to pull on outer clothing, and taking charge he said;

'I'll report to the bridge. Meanwhile, get yourselves dressed and be prepared to search everywhere.'

He reported the loss to Ian, who told him to rouse the bosun and organise two search parties to sweep the port and starboard well-decks from end to end. Ian phoned down to Mr Michaels who was soon on the upper bridge. Told that Wilkie and the bosun were organising search parties, he nodded and said:

'They'll do a good job. Let's hope they find him. And, if they don't … well. I'm afraid that he's gone. We'd never find him in this weather and anyway, we couldn't leave the convoy.'

Very quickly two teams of men linked arms and clung to rigging and scoured every nook and cranny along the length of the ship. One moment the water was around their ankles, the next it was waist high. The Old Man waited in the chartroom for news and finally had to call off the search. Some of the searchers were dropping with exhaustion and cold and they still had to go on watch when their time came. The consensus of opinion was that Collins had taken his hand off the lifeline when the *Venetia* lurched, that he was thrown off balance, slipped on the wet flybridge, cracked his head and fell onto the well-deck where, semi-conscious or even unconscious he had been washed overboard. He was well liked and his loss threw a pall of gloom over the entire ship's company.

Later that day the bosun went into the focsle to pack up Collin's belongings to be stowed away and then to be sent to his next of kin. He was stopped by some of the older hands who said that it would be unlucky. His belongings should be left where they were, untouched, until the *Venetia* berthed. Gauging the lie of the land the bosun gave in.

'Old superstitions, boss,' said the mate. They won't touch any of his stuff until we berth alongside and then we can pack it and have it sent to his family.'

His death had one anticipated repercussion. I was still paying two midnight visits a week to the focsle to play chess with Pablo. Smith took it up with me, saying severely that one was enough. He made me promise not to pay any more visits until we reached the Clyde and dropped anchor.

10

THE FINAL LEG

The loss of Collins was felt badly, as if he were a family member, which in a way he was. We wondered how many merchant seamen had died in the pack attack on the convoy. Several hundred, certainly. It was bruited that eleven ships in our convoy had been sunk, and after we scattered it was likely that the U-boats had picked off helpless independents. At that time the merchant seamen knew that the Battle of the Atlantic was going very badly; the losses could be concealed from the public but not from those in the thick of the war at sea. There were too many survivors from the devastated convoys with time on their hands in seamen's missions and YMCAs who exchanged experiences and knowledge. None faulted the Royal Navy for their losses, knowing that they were too thinly stretched and doing their damndest. When they hauled seamen from the water, from rafts and boats they went beyond the call of duty in their care of them, and relations between the two services were very close.

As we steamed into the North Minch the temperature dropped sharply and a treacherous thin film of ice coated the entire ship. Walking became hazardous and tumbles were frequent. I coped by hanging onto supports and walking as flat-footed as I could with all my weight coming down on my front foot. Protective RAF surveillance overhead was almost continuous. We passed two lifeboats tied to one another; they were empty. No ships stopped to pick them up.

The food reached an all time low, but no one seemed particularly bothered about it. Most of the inedible servings were thrown into the waters. Each ship supported its own cloud of shrieking gulls. With the green coastline of the Isles of Lewis and Harris sliding past our starboard, we were all cloaked with the illusion of security. We were home. Nothing could happen to us now. All thoughts turned to being ashore, enormous fry-ups and women who could make you forget the tribulations of the sea. Johnny worried me. He was on tenterhooks, paranoid at the thought of not getting leave or seeing his mother. I walked a tightrope of saying nothing to dim his hopes and at the same time trying not to raise them too high.

At 0930 ship's time on 24 February we rounded the south end of the Mull of Kintyre, steamed past Ailsa Craig and turned into the Firth of Clyde. Radio watchkeeping ceased so I stayed on the well-deck and breathed in the invigorating salty air and watched the eastern coast of the Isle of Arran glide by. Our small convoy of survivors had already split up; most of the ships were heading south to unload in Merseyside and Avonmouth. We dropped anchor in Rothesay Bay, a pleasant, small seaside resort. Three vessels were beached, destroyed by enemy action. One had its entire stern blown off.

Two hours later we upped anchor and headed for the gap being opened in the protective boom across the harbour. The *Venetia* was ahead until a Polish freighter belched clouds of black smoke, picked up speed and tried to pass us. Roy glared at it and snorted;

'No you bloody don't,' and voice-tubed the engine room for more revolutions.

'What the hell for?' asked Dai.

'An emergency,' yelled Roy, winking at the helmsman Ginger, who was grinning. 'Don't waste a moment. Just bloody do it!'

Poor Dai must have been wondering what catastrophe was upon

us, but he obliged. We sped forward and the Pole dropped back from level pegging. Both crews shouted and cat-called exuberantly at one another and the bosun observed that it was one way of learning Polish swearwords. Stevey added that it was lucky that the Old Man was busy with his papers otherwise he would have blown a gasket at Roy's frivolity. We moved farther up the Clyde and dropped anchor off Dunoon. I have never seen so many ships, and what staggered me most was the massive size of a whaling ship whose huge steel sides towered over us. Tea was passed around, but it was so foul we all spat it out and threw the rest at passing gulls. The evening meal was just as bad and I left it untouched on the saloon table. I bumped into Wilkie later and told him about it.

'You should have seen what we were served up,' he said. 'Still, we're home and I'll sign off this bastard. Hungry, Sparky?'

'Not half.'

Thirty minutes later Johnny, Wilkie and I were having tea and toast in my cabin. Wilkie exerted an undeniable influence over Maltese Johnny and Einstein. I learned later that some of the focsle blamed the cook for their hunger and wanted to take their anger out on him, but Wilkie protected him, for which Maltese Johnny was grateful.

We both tried to assure Johnny that he was so close to home that he was bound to get compassionate leave. The same night the mate spoke to him and Johnny threw his hands up with delight. The next morning, well before dawn, I watched him clamber down into a small boat and he was rowed to shore. I waved to him with my fingers crossed; his joy was mixed with a lot of trepidation.

An air of expansive relaxation spread throughout the *Venetia*. This was it. We had survived. We were across. We could sleep in pyjamas and walk around with being encumbered with neck-breakers and panic. We gazed contentedly at the green hills sloping backwards from the still grey waters and the scattered cottages sending homely wisps of smoke up to mottled skies and we felt lucky. Both outward and homeward bound we had gotten away with it. The mate eased up on finding work for idle hands and many made up for lost sleep.

Three days passed at anchor. No mail arrived and the food reached its lowest ebb. The chief steward warned that clean linen and towels would have to be used that much longer; replenishments had not arrived, not even fresh food and water. We wanted to be rid of our cargo and began to fidget at living on top of it. The fourth morning Mr Michaels and the chief engineer went ashore. In Greenock they took a taxi to the company offices in Glasgow and did not phone beforehand, not wanting to be fobbed off over the wire. The company manager was there but did not know the ship's final destination and discharge point, as he was waiting for Admiralty orders.

The chief engineer gave a blunt résumé of the state of the *Venetia*'s engines and a list of vital replacement parts. He was told the matter would be seen to, but the chief demanded to know which items would be delivered and when. The manager pointed that there was a war on, to which the engineer replied that he would never have known. In his turn Mr Michaels kicked up the dust over the non-delivery of mail and its bad effect on the crew. The manager promised to give the mail priority attention, but all in all it was not a happy session. When the two men returned to the ship they looked their ages, crumpled and weary.

The next morning started badly. Shore leave, or the lack of it, had superseded food as the hot topic. At breakfast, attended by Mr Michaels, the mate, Roy, Smith and myself, the mate noted that the men were very sullen and that there was talk of them calling one of the many small boats in the harbour and bribing the boatmen to take them ashore. This was not an uncommon occurrence in busy ports when men who had been ship-bound for many weeks snapped at being cooped up at anchor for days on end. In some cases this resulted in seamen missing sailings when their ships received immediate departure orders. They would then have to report to the nearest British consul, receive a pittance of money for which they would sign and repay later, and be shipped home as a DBS (Distressed British Seaman).

The inevitable happened. Two hours later Wilkie led a deputation of five along the flybridge up to the lower bridge deck. They hung back. It struck me that Wilkie could have managed as well without them. Stevey opened the captain's door and shut it hastily behind him.

'Do yourself a favour and go away,' he said to Wilkie. 'He's had a sleepless night.'

Too late. Mr Michaels appeared. He told Stevey to go back in and get on with his cleaning, then glared at Wilkie and growled irascibly.

'What is it now, sir? The food? Shore leave? Both? If it is food, fresh provisions will be aboard later today. I can get no information about when we sail and where to. However, I have decided to take it on my own shoulders to issue twelve shore passes for today. A boat will here at midday sharp. Be back at midnight at the latest. Meanwhile, Mr Parkinson will go into Greenock this afternoon and telephone the company, and if there is no promise of movement I will issue twelve more passes. But I must emphasise that you must be back by midnight in case we receive sailing orders for tomorrow.'

Mr Michaels returned to his quarters, slamming the door behind him. Ernie Jenkins, a Huddersfield greaser, said that it was not good enough. He stirred up Jean Callou, who only had getting to his girlfriend on his mind. Wilkie gave him a mock bow, stepped aside and told him to pursue the matter himself.

Shore passes. Gold dust. To my delight Smith was given one, which he in turn gave to me. Chippy, the bosun, Arne the Danish greaser, Dai, Wilkie, Derek Kenny, Ginger, Mandel, two greasers and Billy Boy received the others. Dai approached me and suggested that we go ashore together, which we did. When the boat landed us at Greenock, the bosun and Chippy headed straight for a pub. Dai and I caught a quick train to Glasgow station. We had both drawn money and we decided to pool it and whatever was left at the end we would divide fifty-fifty. We were both starving and we slipped into the North British Hotel for a first class meal. Dai called it a 'very classy hotel'. We were very comfortable with one another and conversation never flagged. I was the first Jew Dai had ever engaged in easy dialogue and he was intensely curious about my religion and family life. After our second coffee our talk turned to other things.

'I hate these Mickey Mouse leaves,' said Dai. 'The ones where we have a day ashore and all the time is spent looking at the clock because no sooner are we on land that it's time to go back.' I wondered whether all who came ashore would return to the *Venetia*. 'You bet your arse,' said Dai. 'Every day they're adrift they'll lose five shillings pay. Anyway, what shall we do now? Cinema? Sightsee? Drink? Just walk? There must be something more exciting. Hang on ...' He walked across to the reception desk and returned looking like the cat who's had the cream. 'Bingo, Sparky. Ballroom dancing at a place called the Locarno. It costs sixpence to go in and finishes at six o'clock.'

The Locarno was packed with servicemen from every service in every Allied nation. There were girls and married women galore, and the six-piece band was good. Dai and I were in civvies, which was a big mistake. Time and time again it was commented on by women to whom uniforms ruled, the more exotic the more the pulling power. Still, we took up with two pretty sisters after Dai whispered to them that I had survived twenty-eight days in an open boat and I told them that Dai had been torpedoed three times, all being fair in love and war.

Later we spent time in a pub, then we had some food. We were continually aware of the Damoclean sword of passing time. The sisters were in the market for a film or even another dance, but Dai stared at me and tapped his watch. I plucked up courage and told them that we had to get back to our ship. Dai muttered disconsolately on the bus back to Greenock:

'God, it became frosty when you opened your mouth, Sparky. Bloody hell. We could have scored tonight. I know I shan't be able to sleep.'

Back on ship I went to bed feeling very frustrated and fed up. Yet, it was a pleasant night, starry and clear, and as I stared across at the other ships, I mellowed. It was all so peaceful. I lay on my bunk and read a little, then fell asleep. I was wakened about three o'clock, my honed antennae picking up trouble in the offing. Shouts and raucous laughter came from the direction of the focsle, growing louder and louder. The tone was ugly and I could distinguish the voices of Ginger, Charlie Smith, Derek Kenny and others.

'We'll do the bastards.'

'Aye, and that bloody Twitch and Maltese Johnny.'

'He's ashore.'

'Lucky for him.'

'What did that fat old cow say to us in the tavern?' The voice scaled up with mimicry. 'You merchant seamen get better paid than my George in the army. And he's risking his life all the time.' The voice reverted to flat Yorkshire. 'Aye. Her George should have seen her laying out her wares for sale like kippers on a fishmonger's slab.'

More drunken laughter, too loud, too close. I sat upright. Violence was in the air. Before I could swing my legs over the bunkboard my door crashed open and Wilkie burst in. He reeked of whisky and was jacketless. His chest heaved beneath a stained shirt unbuttoned all the way down to his waist. Unkempt hair stranded across his dank forehead above angry bloodshot eyes and he swayed as he clutched a half-empty bottle of Black and White whisky. He belched twice and thrust the bottle at me.

'Have a drink on me, Sparky,' he ordered. I shook my head and said that I did not drink. Wrong move. An able seaman behind Wilkie raised his hand in a drinking motion and nodded to me. Later he told me that he was warning me not to cross Wilkie in that mood.

But I was too bemused and afraid to think straight, and an inherent streak of stubbornness made me decline. Wilkie's right arm shot out and grabbed my shoulder; his left hand tightened around the bottle's neck. 'So, Sparky, even you think you're too bloody high and mighty to drink with a focsle rat.'

He did not seem to be the same man who had made tea and toast and chatted with Johnny and myself. I took the bottle and put it to my mouth, tilting it as if drinking. Instead, I spread my tongue against the opening to block the liquid, but it was a mistake as it made whisky spill down my chin. He saw through the ploy and for one fraught minute I thought he was going to hit me.

'Don't play games with me, lad,' he said. 'I like you better than the others but if you try to fool me I'll hurt you.'

I nodded and sipped from the bottle. It was my first taste of whisky and I spluttered and choked. Wilkie nodded approval. There was a sudden commotion in the doorway, a milling around and then Chippy burst into my cabin. Without a word he pushed himself between Wilkie and myself, took Wilkie's hand from my shoulder and took the bottle. I later learned that it was Long John who had fetched him, not liking what he saw. Chippy spoke to Wilkie, who was quickly sobering up, and there was a chance that it might have all passed off quickly but for two developments. Firstly, the chief steward, who had been burning the midnight oil with Mr Michaels, descended to the lower bridge and pushed through some seamen. One hit him and another slammed him hard against a bulkhead, calling him a money-grubbing bastard.

Secondly, as Wilkie was being urged out into the alleyway by Chippy, Mr Michaels appeared in full uniform. The mob around the chief steward parted before him, but his presence incensed Wilkie and the balloon went up. It was all so quick and confusing I can only record what I saw from my position on the bunk where I finished up on my back fending off bodies with my feet, although no one was taking any notice of me by then. Wilkie threw a punch at the Old Man, at which Chippy hauled him away back into the cabin, the Captain following. Charlie Smith tried to pull him back but the bosun appeared and grabbed Charlie in a headlock. The chief steward took advantage of the men's change of interest and scurried to his cabin, locking himself in. Stevey appeared, shouting at the men to come to their senses and make themselves scarce. But many were in a belligerent mood and Stevey found himself trading punches in self defence. The whisky bottle dropped to the deck and smashed, releasing the overpowering smell of alcohol.

Gradually, between them, Chippy, Mr Michaels and Stevey pushed Wilkie out into the alleyway, and I saw Mr Michaels clutch his wrist and curse.

'Damn and blast you, sir. You have smashed my watch.'

The struggle moved out of my cabin and I sat and looked blearily at the wreckage; my sink was smashed. Then I heard more shouting, and I slid onto the desk in my stockinged feet. Everybody seemed to be lining the lower bridge rails. I joined them and was startled to see four policemen on board and a police launch bobbing about at the foot of the gangway. Wilkie, bloodstained and dishevelled, was between two of them. He was handcuffed. A police sergeant was talking with Mr Michaels and Chippy, and Stevey was nursing a black eye.

Later that day Wilkie was charged with various offences, and we heard that the case was going to the High Court. Early in the morning the police returned and took statements, including one from me. My cabin presented a most dismal sight; blood stained the white settee cover, a kick had smashed the side of the chest of drawers, clothes, books and papers had been trampled into a sodden mess. I slept well; the hanging whisky fumes must have helped.

I was awoken by Johnny, returned from shore leave. He commented that it looked like I'd had an orgy. Standing behind him was Smith, boggling at the mess. I tried to explain but they already knew the details. Smith threw me a copy of the *Glasgow Citizen* which had reports of more bombings on London; the East End had taken the most punishment. It made me feel very guilty because I had forgotten to phone home while ashore.

The mate took the unusual step of visiting the focsle to talk to the men. He told them that many deserved fining for a variety of offences, but that Mr Michaels was inclined to overlook last night. He added that any further trouble would be punished as severely as possible. Everyone was very subdued and Roy expressed all our sentiments when he asked God to let the *Venetia* sail and finally put this voyage to rest.

Everyone was very good about my cabin; four focsle men came up and shamefacedly offered to lend me a hand cleaning it up. I thanked them but declined. I learned that Maltese Johnny had gone ashore two days earlier for medical treatment, and had been replaced by a man called George Testrall. He was in his fifties and from Maidstone, lean but obviously enjoyed his trade. It was reported that Maltese Johnny had contracted gonorrhoea in Aruba, which confused the crew.

'Blimey, he was only ashore a couple of hours. Where did he find her?'

'Dunno, but I bet he wishes he hadn't.'

Johnny and Stevey helped me clean out my cabin. Chippy repaired the chest of drawers and with the aid of Dai repaired the sink and fixed it firmly back against the bulkhead. The chief steward issued me with fresh towels, soap, a tube of toothpaste and a whisky-free blanket. That evening the mate opened the conversation at supper.

'Do you want the good news or the bad news first?'

'The good,' said Roy quickly. 'I'm sick of the bad.'

'Right. We're sailing tomorrow morning. But we'll discharge in the Thames.'

The news that we were going to carry our cargo right round Scotland and down to the Thames was greeted with dismay. It seemed to be tempting providence. As we set off and steamed down the Firth of Clyde, other ships appeared as if from nowhere to join us. Three were tankers, which explained why they, like us, were being sent south. That was where the air war was fiercest and the RAF needed our fuel. Just before we sailed a representative of the company came alongside in a small launch. He spent half an hour with Mr Michaels, and when he left he took the belongings of Collins, Wilkie and Maltese Johnny. It was a sad sight.

Monday 30 September saw the *Venetia* one of a long file of merchantmen rounding the Mull of Kintyre. We sported our red B flag, denoting our dangerous cargo, as did the other tankers. Spitfires and Hurricanes, here we come! Later that day we formed a large convoy of some twenty-five vessels, but as half were in ballast we knew that when we and the other loaded ships cleared the North Minch and headed eastwards around Cape Wrath the others would be directed to join a trans-Atlantic convoy.

We were back on full radio watch and the distress file began to thicken. Two ships were torpedoed off the Faroes and another went down off Rockall. The skull and crossbones flags that U-boats flew recording triumphs when they returned to home bases must have kept some German flag-maker busy. Our old friend GBR Rugby was still hard at work, advising ships to avoid certain areas, reporting a Luftwaffe attack on a convoy off the Norfolk coast and warning of E-boat activity on the east coast.

A terrible storm blew up as we passed Strathy Point and suddenly the ships in the convoy were floundering and struggling and yawing; station-keeping became impossible. As dusk fell, fearful of collisions, ships' masters pulled away outwards and that night some of us were so far apart we could have been classified as sailing independently. The *Venetia* was digging her forepeak under huge waves so deeply that the seas swept back over the well-deck and sometimes over the flybridge itself. Focsle hands changing over watch keeping left the focsle in pairs, lashed to one another by rope and both holding grimly onto the lifeline. I had resumed my visits to Pablo but I cried off until the weather abated. All that night the *Venetia* acted the submarine, half under water and half on top. Come daylight we were alone. The wind abated but from massive low black clouds came heavy rain. Mr Michaels maintained the course set and we rolled and tumbled our way towards Pentland Firth.

'Bloody Scots weather,' growled Roy. 'It turns corners and hits you in the back of the neck.'

It was no place to be alone and the men's anxiety was apparent. At noon a Sunderland Short flying boat circled low overhead and signalled with her aldis lamp to our bridge. It informed us that our scattered convoy was some ten miles ahead and reforming, and that we should catch up. There was the inevitable altercation over the voice tube between the deck officers who wanted more speed, and the engineers who said it could not be done. The bridge had its way and it was a good moment when our monkey-island lookout reported ships ahead. We closed and could eventually count the other eleven ships which had turned east round Cape Wrath with us. Our escort was a corvette and two armed traders, one of which stayed at our tail, both to protect and pick up survivors.

The North Sea weather stayed vile. Our speed was reduced, but that afternoon, Thursday 3 October, we straggled into the Firth of Forth and dropped anchor. We wondered how long we would stay, as there was a terrible itch amongst the men to pay off and get ashore. That night we heard air raid sirens wailing ashore.

'U-boat attack on army barracks,' quipped Stevey.

The next morning Mr Michaels was taken ashore by a naval launch. He attended a convoy conference and the same afternoon we sailed. Turning south past Bass Rock we formed two long columns of naval vessels, fifteen in each column. We were eighth down the coastside column. It was a black night with heavy rain. Roy was on watch when the *Venetia* nearly cut down a fishing smack; he was alerted by the bump when it hit the *Venetia*'s side and heard shouts and whistles. He raced to the starboard wing and was just in time to see the smack slithering out of sight. He sighed, returned to the chartroom for a quiet smoke and wondered which British port would be most likely to furnish him with a signing-on for Sydney.

After my watch I breakfasted with Roy and Johnny. We were all in a happy mood. A combination of fresh provisions, a better cook and the nearness of journey's end all help, and we all tacitly agreed that the improvement was due in great part to Wilkie, his persistence and the episode off Greenock. But no one spoke of him now, nor Collins.

A sudden explosion stiffened us with shock. Roy hared out onto the well-deck and we followed. The first vessel in the seaside column, a British carrying general cargo and timber loaded in Vancouver, had hit a mine. The strike had broken her back and as we passed her she was settling fast by the stern and her bows were rising in that slow fatal arc towards the vertical. Timber baulks, a raft, oil drums and other debris were slipping into the seas. Men were sliding down into the starboard boat which had been lowered. Fuel oil was spreading on the surface of the water, a treacly, lethal blanket. The naval trawler at the rear of the convoy was steaming up fast to pick up survivors. From that moment our progress seemed very slow. Would the Yorkshire coast never end? Would we never lose sight of Flamborough head?

On radio watch we picked up blues, more torpedoing and a straightforward SOS from a powerless and probably overloaded vessel foundering in severe North Atlantic gales. The commodore warned all ships to keep a sharp lookout for E-boats in the run into the Thames. They did not appear; many armed trawlers were about. A sizeable northbound convoy passed our seaward side, all in ballast, all destined for the Americas and beyond to collect cargoes.

On Saturday 5 October we dropped anchor in the Thames. Johnny and I were leaning on the well-deck rail staring at the pier and shore. He had not spoken about leave with his widowed mother, and I asked no questions. But he was still the best of companions and we could lean side by side without talking and feel completely at ease with one another. Stevey joined us and mused upon the delights of Southend: the cockles and mussels, the oysters and jellied eels, the fish and chips and candy floss and, naturally, the Southend 'talent'. That night we watched searchlights pattern the sky as German planes flew overhead bound for London. I saw the flashes in the distance and the glow thrown up by fires. I could not wait to get ashore and telephone my family.

On Sunday we weighed anchor and proceeded independent from the convoy up the Thames. Barrage balloons stretched skywards as if seeking the sun through the thick dark cloud. It was the same old river, brown, muddy and littered with driftwood. As it narrowed, individual landmarks appeared. I took up my cap and looked at it. It had barely been worn and I jumped on it and rubbed it against the bulkhead to take the newness out of it. Johnny brought me a mug of tea, and then, we were there. The *Venetia* slowed and I saw the storage tanks on shore. The engines ceased to vibrate and the anchor was dropped. The telegraph rang 'finished with engines'. Suddenly all became very quiet and peaceful. And strangely melancholy.

On shore I telephoned home. Apart from a few windows smashed by blasts and roof tiles loosened, all was well.

I then called Marconi International Marine Company at their East Ham office, as per instructions. They had told me to report to them within forty-eight hours. They had another ship for me, the MV *Hylton*, owned by Souters of Newcastle on Tyne, and it was sailing from Middlesborough. Johnny was there with me and was watching my face.

'Not coming back, Sparky?'

'No.' We were both silent and I said, 'come on, you greedy bugger, I'll buy you a meal.'

It was a full English breakfast and I forked my sausage and bacon onto Johnny's plate. He laughed. It was a poignant parting as we had become very close. We promised to keep in touch.

The *Hylton* took me up to Vancouver, a long trip stretched out by the odd mishap. Leaving Bermuda in a homebound convoy, we were hit by a hurricane and forced to limp into Halifax in Nova Scotia for refitting. After three weeks there we sailed for home, were torpedoed just south of Iceland, picked up by the corvette HMS *Dianella* and landed in Londonderry, a voyage I later wrote about in my book *Atlantic Roulette*. At home there was only one card from Johnny, from Curaçao. I telephoned Gow, Harrison and Company and spoke to the manager. After my answers to his questions satisfied him that I was who I said I was, I asked;

'How and where is Johnny Walters?'

There was a long pause.

'Sorry, son,' he said, 'you won't be hearing from Johnny Walters again.'

'Never?'

'Never.'

Never before or since have I shed tears in a red telephone box.

INDEX